Oh, BLEEP!
I Lost My Job

*An Insider's Guide
to Job Search*

Published by HenschelHAUS Publishing, Inc.
Milwaukee, Wisconsin
www.henschelHAUSbooks.com

Cover design by Julie Quirk,
Email: juliecookquirk@ yahoo.com

ISBN: 978159598-940-6
E-ISBN: 978159598-941-3
LCCN: 2022952064

Printed in the United States of America

Oh, BLEEP!
I Lost My Job

An Insider's Guide to Job Search

Richard J. Longabaugh

Henschel
HAUS
www.henschelHAUSbooks.com

Milwaukee, Wisconsin

Table of Contents

Section 4—Approaching the Finish Line

About This Book

Job loss is painful, traumatic, frustrating, depressing, bewildering, and a whole lot more. This book deals with the emotional and practical aspects of looking for a new job. Just as the realities of job loss can be brutal, this book doesn't gloss over what it's going to take to rejoin the workforce—on your own terms. Don't expect vanilla soft-serve as you read, nor is this a three-, or five-, or twelve-step program to a new job. To be sure, job search is a rough road and you must realize you can't travel it alone. Emotional patience and disciplined practice are essential. This book will help you learn those skills and more on your way to becoming a successful job seeker. On the other hand, things don't have to be all that bleak. You may come to realize that losing your job was actually the best thing that could have happened to you.

Ready? Read on.

Acknowledgements

There are a number of individuals and organizations who need to be thanked for their support and guidance to me, and for their selfless commitment to helping those in job search.

First, and foremost, is 40Plus of Southeastern Wisconsin, a networking group that has been offering advice to job seekers since 1976. Other groups include:

- Lumen Christi Employment Network (Mequon, WI)
- Crossroads Career REACH Support Ministry (Hales Corners, WI)
- Professional Opportunities Networking Group (Pewaukee, WI)

There are many individuals who have helped me along the way and to whom I am indebted, including Ellie Mixter-Keller, Pat Cronin, Dennis Cherne, Carol Schober, Peter Wick, Jim Lysaught, Sue Gresham, Jeff Perceval, Wayne Breitbarth, Jodi Castagnozzi, Kira Henschel, Julie Quirk, Sara Junio, Debra Rudan, Robert Bachman, and other 40Plus Board Members. My apologies to others I have neglected because book writing, like job search, is not a solo endeavor.

Preface

Oh, BLEEP!

Offended? Get over it. You have bigger problems. You've lost your job!

Job loss is one of life's most disruptive events. There are plenty of friends or family members who will be glad to commiserate with you in your time of loss, but their sympathy is short-lived and their emotional support is ephemeral.

This book is intended to help the job seeker get through the grieving, recovery, and heavy lifting necessary to find new employment. The approaches taken in this book may be blunt, perhaps controversial, unconventional, and not long on sympathy. Nice and easy will not work.

The reason is simple. The soft approach to job search is doomed to failure. Sports analogies notwithstanding, job search demands coaching and practice.

This book is the result of the experiences and counseling that come from working with hundreds of job seekers for more than a dozen years and a similar number of years as a retained search headhunter. The advice is based on my own experiences and may conflict with that of other coaches and experts.

If you are serious about finding a new job, you will be successful. The reality is, however, it will probably take longer than you think and there is no surefire, one way to job nirvana. You may need to do some things out of your comfort zone like asking for help, networking, or using technology in ways previously foreign to you, such as LinkedIn or Zoom. The principles in job search seem to change every couple of years, so if you do not learn some of these new ways, do not expect to be successful.

This book is not intended to be all things for everyone seeking a new job. There are subject matter experts and other resources that do a better job in their respective areas of expertise than I do in this book. This is also the case that the pace of change in topics, particularly in the area of technology, is too rapid to keep up. Therefore, it is incumbent on you, the job seeker, to do the serious work in job search.

It is often said in networking meetings that if you only get one good idea out of a session, then it was worth your time. I hope you do get at least one good idea from this book. While I think there are more than a few good ideas in what follows, there are several spots in the book where I will **Caution, Secret Tip, Note,** and **Quick Tip** you. These are worthy of your particular attention.

You should also see that we have provided pages for you to make notes. Please feel free to underline, highlight, and otherwise mark up this book. This is not a coffee table tome that just sits and looks pretty. Make it your workbook so it can truly work for you.

One final thought. Is job loss a blessing? Think about it and read on.

—Rich Longabaugh

Section 1
The Beginning

1. The Boot

Oh, BLEEP!

It can happen any one of a dozen ways—a call to come to the conference room, an invitation to join your boss with someone from HR (like Heather), an unscheduled meeting with the boss, perhaps an elegant lunch. The result is the same: Fired. Separated. Released. Downsized. You're gone. Done. You've gotten *The Boot*.

Maybe this is something you have seen coming because you have a keen sense of business conditions or you have survived other rounds of lay-offs. On the other hand, the news may have come out of the blue or you may have been completely blindsided. Your reaction could be physical and/or emotional. Shock or disbelief are common. If this is starting to sound like the well-known steps of grief, you are not far off; more on grieving later in this book.

Even though the US economy has seen millions of workers laid off, job loss is personal. The goal of this book is to help you deal with the very real emotional aspects of losing employment while equipping you with tools and tactics to become reemployed.

NEGOTIATING THE DEPARTURE

As a newly released, or fired, employee, you need to understand the company has "a plan." After all, they've been considering your departure longer than have you. Not surprisingly, their plan is infinitely better than anything you might come up with on the spot. What should you do? Read on.

When you have "the meeting," it is generally in the employer's interest to get you out of the building as quickly as possible. Once the decision has been made to let you go, you become a liability on many levels. At best, your presence can have a toxic impact on the remaining staff. Other than an occasional sympathetic coworker, you will be shunned and no one wants to hang around you if you get emotional or cry.

At worst, there is a fear that you may react badly to the news and take revenge on the company in the form of sabotage, unpleasant outbursts, or poisoning the well with customers or other employees. You may be asked to leave immediately (sometimes with an escort to the front door) or given a brief moment to gather your personal items (under the watchful eye of HR). You probably don't feel you are in a position to do much about it.

DON'T BE A WIMP

What's the worst they can do? You've already been fired. You need to gather your wits about you as quickly as possible and start to negotiate your separation. If you can't manage to discuss your new status before you hit the street (perfectly understandable), ask to come back in the morning or perhaps after hours to negotiate the terms of your departure. Easier said than done and most newly fired employees often think they don't have any leverage in this situation.

Wrong.

Most employers, particularly larger or union-based companies, will have policies governing terminations. Remember, they have "a plan."

Sometimes, in smaller companies, or if you are the only one being let go, they may be more inclined to negotiate. After all, they are usually feeling badly about the situation and are susceptible to short-term steps to make this less painful for them.

Remember: this is all about them. Your years of loyal service, family situation, or unique circumstances are really not their concern. However, this doesn't mean you shouldn't try to take advantage of their guilt.

DO NOT sign anything. Some employers may try to strong-arm you into signing a separation agreement. You can be sure of one thing—this is not in your best interest. How could something they wrote be in your favor? Ask to take a copy home for review. When in doubt, seek advice from a labor attorney. Yes, the lawyer will probably send you a bill, but the advice is worth having and the bill may be tax deductible as a job-searching expense.

QUESTIONS YOU SHOULD ASK OR NEGOTIATE:

- How long will I stay on the payroll?

- When do I have to leave—one hour, one day, one month? *The longer you can stay on the payroll, the better.*

- Will I get paid for unused vacation, personal days, sick days?

- What about my bonus? *Try to negotiate a pro-rated payout at a minimum.*

- How long will my benefits continue? *Some employers may extend benefits longer than salary.*

- Will I get an agreement on commissions earned but not paid?

- Did you get a letter of separation? *Get a written statement as to the reasons for your dismissal.*

- Will the company give you a positive reference? *While most employers instruct the HR staff to provide minimal information, letters of reference or commendation should be gathered before leaving.*

- Do you have access to your personnel file? *Get copies of performance reviews (if you haven't kept them over the years.)*

- Will the employer contest unemployment?

- Will I receive outplacement assistance?

- Am I eligible for re-entry / re-hire rights?

- Will I have a salary continuation agreement?

- Are you clear about your 401(k), pension, stock or other deferred benefits?

> **Note:**
> **Keep your emotions under control.**
> **There is nothing to be gained by having**
> **a crying fit or throwing things around**
> **your cubicle.**

Again, if you can't manage to discuss these items before you hit the street, retreat and regroup and ask to come back at another time to negotiate the terms of your departure.

Your personal integrity and the manner in which you conducted yourself after getting this shock will leave a lasting impression with people you may later want to speak on your behalf.

Quick Tips:

- It's not personal, but you're done.

- Negotiate your departure.

- Don't be shy.

- Don't lose your cool.

Notes and Ideas

2. Getting a Grip

You've gotten *The Boot.* Now what? You have to tell your family. This can be one of the most difficult and stressful conversations you are likely to have.

Don't avoid it. Regardless of family circumstances, past history, personal style, or fear, suck it up and discuss things as soon as possible.

Undoubtedly, the immediate concern is financial. Do not panic. Sit down with your spouse, roommate, or others and review your income and expense prospects for the next six to twelve months, under-estimating income and over-estimating expenses. Look at everything and be realistic.

It may be prudent to cut back on discretionary expenses but don't overreact and cut critical expenses like insurance policies. Plan to discuss your new circumstances with your banker, lawyer, accountant, or investment advisor. Good planning at this stage can minimize stress down the road.

Figure out now what you will need in a new job offer. This may sound premature but once you get into an interview situation, you don't want to sound unprepared when asked about salary and other benefits. Perhaps your circumstances have changed. For example, you need better health insurance, or the kids may be out of college, or you need a stronger 401k. Bottom line, the compensation package at your old employer may not reflect your current or future needs. Be ready for those negotiations.

Now, what are you going to tell other people? Hiding is not a good strategy, as most people will find out sooner or later. You may feel slighted, wronged, or humiliated but those are emotions you can learn to manage. You didn't do anything wrong. In most cases, it was a circumstance beyond your control.

Any news or information is best coming from you. Come up with a public statement (see **Exit Statement** in Chapter 21) or a one-liner to address your temporary situation. The good news is that everyone knows someone who has lost a job. Your situation, while unfortunate and personally tragic, is not unique. You will not have to do much explaining.

Holidays are particularly stressful for the unemployed. Normally, most of us spend more time than usual with friends and family during holiday periods. Unless you plan to avoid all such gatherings (a horribly flawed strategy, by the way), you need to be prepared to talk about your situation.

Aunt Betty may coo all over you while Uncle Joe, emboldened by too much holiday cheer, chides you for getting a useless sociology degree in the first place.

Friends' reactions will cover a broad spectrum. How you handle these situations will depend a) on your overall emotional health and, b) what you actually say about your temporary status. You do have the power to control what others say.

Now is also a good time to start amassing your tool kit to equip you for the job-search journey. There is more detail on this topic later in the book but for the moment, I want to focus on your "head game."

Who you are does not change with your employment circumstance. Most job seekers need to polish up their egos before starting this journey. One way is to look over your past performance evaluations and review your past accomplishments. You are not damaged goods and for many years, companies have sought fit to pay you good money to do a job.

Another way to reinforce your skill set is through personal assessment tools such as Myers-Briggs or DiSC. My personal favorite is ***STRENGTHSFINDER 2.0*** (1) After taking a brief on-line assessment, the result is a listing of your top five strengths. Many job seekers have found the descriptions of these strengths to be an invaluable aid in describing the value they bring to an organization.

QUICK TIPS:
- Don't hide.
- Learn to manage your emotions.
- Develop a one-liner.

RESOURCES:
(1) Don Clifton, STRENGTHSFINDER 2.0, Gallup Press, 2000.

Notes and Ideas

3. Don't Get Started

In case you missed the subtlety of the previous chapter, let me make this point very clear. Unless you have been preparing for your dismissal for some time, you are not ready to undertake a job search!

Whether you realize it or not, inside you is a bundle of knotted emotions that accompany job loss and those need to be allowed to unwind before you are ready to get started. Take a vacation (seriously!), spend time with your family, or start those long-neglected projects around the house. Don't jump into a job search and definitely, do not go on an interview. You aren't ready and at this point, your misplaced enthusiasm will only harm your efforts.

A skilled interviewer will quickly pick up when a candidate is carrying toxic baggage even if he or she doesn't know specifically that it's from job loss. This venom seeps into your answers and makes it nearly impossible for you to gain the upper hand in an interview. Nobody wants to hire someone with attitude problems or an employee who is quick to badmouth his former employer. There are plenty of other candidates who don't bring such ill will to work. Job seekers must purge themselves of any negativity towards their former employer or boss. This comes with time and practice—time to heal from the wounds of past experiences and, practice in saying the right words to answer interviewers' questions.

By now, this advice may sound redundant, but job loss, particularly after long-term employment, is a major life event. It may not be as profound as a family death or divorce but the emotional impact should not be under-emphasized or ignored.

The loss of income, community or industry status, sense of self-worth, or feelings of failure are very real and must be addressed. I often refer to this as "arrows in the back" or the "grieving period." As with any other life crisis, to pretend it doesn't bother you or to ignore it are forms of denial. Psychologists will tell you that unless you deal with these feelings, they can become disruptive and cause very real problems.

GRIEVING

While this book is not a psychological text, I have included enough references to the mental state of the job seeker to highlight its importance. In many respects, job loss subjects its recipient to personal trauma and emotional stress that can resemble grieving. The seminal work on grieving was developed by Elisabeth Kubler-Ross with the publishing of her book, *On Death and Dying*, released in 1969.

Kubler-Ross developed the five stages of grief as a model to help survivors cope with death and bereavement. (Please see Appendix I.) They are: denial, anger, bargaining, depression, and acceptance. Do any of the following sound familiar to what you experienced when you were let go?

- *Denial:* "No, this can't be happening. I'm too valuable to the company. I've been here for 22 years."

- *Anger:* "Damn company. I knew they were screwed up and my boss is a jackass."

- *Bargaining:* "Can I go part-time? Can I transfer? How long can I stay?"

- *Depression:* "I'll never find another job. I'll never make as much money. I'm a failure."

- *Acceptance:* "Okay. I guess that's that. I'm ready to move on."

This is not to say all these stages are present in everyone who suffers job loss. However, there is enough anecdotal evidence to suggest that most job seekers do go through some form of grieving. You may recognize some of these symptoms in you or someone you know. Don't ignore these signs, but take heart. For most seekers, this is temporary. If you have reason to suspect that job loss is having an effect on your mental well-being, do yourself and your family a favor and contact a physician.

There is no prescription for how long it might take someone to get through the grieving process. Dr. David Kessler, world-renowned expert on grief, a collaborator of Kubler-Ross, and author of *Finding Meaning: The Sixth Stage of Grief,* says:

> "Whenever I talk about the stages of grief, I have to remind people that the stages aren't linear and may not happen in this order." He notes, "(A)cceptance, as you might imagine, is where the power lies. We find control in acceptance."

The good news is that it will be obvious to your job-search colleagues or accountability group (see Chapter 5) when you are through grieving. Do a reality check and ask them. If you can speak dispassionately about your previous employer while focusing on your accomplishments, then maybe you're ready for the show.

Based on the hundreds of group networking sessions I have moderated, it is readily apparent when someone is not ready for the search. The group will ask a newcomer a series of questions like, "How long have you been unemployed?" "How long have you been searching?" How did you lose your job?" We'll give the newbie plenty of time to talk and sometimes vent. If it's only been a week or two, most certainly, he or she is not ready.

Some of the tell-tale signs someone is not ready are:

- If the candidate does not have crisp, concise answers to the questions;

- Hems and haws in her answers or;

- Speaks poorly of the former boss or company.

Dan G.'s early experience comes to mind. The day after his dismissal, he was on the phone trying to line up interviews with some of his former vendors. Most did not return his call but of the two who did, one agreed to meet with him. Upon reflection, Dan acknowledged that during the meeting, most of the questions were about internal policies and relationships at his former employer. He thought candor was his friend and remembers saying things like, "Well, you know how they play politics" and "I never trusted that S.O.B." After leaving the interview, Dan never heard from the vendor again. Lesson learned.

Take comfort from the fact that when you reach out to people, they are inclined to help. They may not know what to do or say, but they are unlikely to refuse your call.

> **Caution:**
> **When it comes to immediate family and spouse, keep your expectations in check.**
> **(See Chapter 5.)**

Quick Tips:

- Don't jump into your job search too quickly.

- Acknowledge the grief/loss.

- Be careful what you say and to whom.

Notes and Ideas

4. The Roller-Coaster Ride

Okay, here's one of many warnings you are going to get. Strap on your big boy/big girl shorts.

The journey you are about to begin will be neither short nor easy. Prepare yourself for a 6-month to 12-month (or longer) process. If it takes less time to find a job, celebrate, because the simple fact is that it will probably take longer than you think. One commonly heard measure is that it takes a month of searching for every $10,000 to $15,000 in salary. You do the math.

There are many metaphors to describe this adventure but one that bears remembering is that of a marathon. Most of us can probably make it 100 yards (walking or running) without dying. However, if you want to run 26 miles, you will need months of preparation, training, and coaching.

At the start of your job search, you need to come to grips with another critical truth. Finding a new job is an emotional roller-coaster ride—it takes work to get to the top of the track and once there, the down ride is an uncontrolled, emotional freefall. One of the hardest tasks you will discover is managing your own emotions.

Probably the most important quality you will need to master is patience. There will be many times when you will be waiting for answers that never come, calls that are never returned, and letters that are never acknowledged. Lacking patience, you will go crazy.

Long and hard do not necessarily mean joyless. While it may not seem the case at the beginning, many veterans of job search report that getting *The Boot* was the best thing that could have happened to them. *Really?*

Think beyond the moment.

- What controlled when you got up in the morning?

- When you left the house?

- When you got home?

- When you were able to take vacations?

- How much time you had for family, friends?

- How much time or money you could contribute to worthy causes?

- What education, training, or certifications you pursued?

Your job!

Perhaps you are one of those truly fortunate individuals who loved your job and can't think of anything else you'd rather do. However, did you work at the last job because you needed the money or profile or social position that came with the gig? Is there something in your heart of hearts that you would rather do, like mission work, teach, or work abroad? Do you want to change careers, not just companies? Were you really happy and personally fulfilled in your last job? The simple fact of being employed sometimes prevents us from considering alternatives.

Now that you have no job, all those constraints have disappeared. Perhaps the financial implications are a bit more problematic but there may also be a new sense of freedom. Think of job loss as a gift that allows you to think, reflect, and act in ways made impossible by having a job.

Karen K. from one of the networking groups, introduced me to the term *"soulbatical."* This manufactured term comes from the world of academia where professors take a sabbatical to write, research, or travel. If you've ever dreamed of getting off the merry-go-round or out of the rat race, this may be your time. Although you did not choose the circumstance, the opportunity or gift is before you. Don't let it slip away.

Caution:
Freedom can be a two-edged sword.

For example, just because you don't have to get up at 6:00 AM to prep and go to work, it doesn't mean you should sleep until 10:00 every day. While that might be okay the first week, it is not a good prescription for someone in job search mode.

While the demands of your old job may have gotten in the way of your true self-expression, there is a potential down side. In partnership with this liberation is an overwhelming need for self-discipline. Like it or not, the demands of the job added structure to your life. Now you have to provide the structure.

Managing your day suddenly becomes a task for which you may not be prepared. Effective time management is a new challenge for many job seekers. If, as the old saying goes, "Tasks expand to fit the time available," you will be amazed to discover days zipping by and you don't know how to account for the time.

One way successful job seekers have found to deal with this potential trap is to keep a log (or time sheet) of where they spend their time each day. This is common practice among professionals like lawyers and accountants who bill by the hour, but it may take practice for the uninitiated. At the end of the week, do the numbers. Where did you spend your time? Review your chart with your accountability group or a fellow searcher and see where you might make changes. Critically examine where the hours went. Was that the best use of your time? Keeping a log or journal can also prepare you for the occasional question from a spouse or relative who wonders how you spend your day.

You should be prepared for something else that is going to happen. You are about to meet a lot of new people. Many of these new faces belong to people you would never have otherwise met. Whether you meet at networking events, an accountability group, an interview, or just down the street, you will come in contact with some extraordinary people who otherwise would never have crossed your path.

Ellen N. told me that while reflecting on her recent 55th birthday, she noted all her close friends who lived in town were at the party. She also said that "with one exception, everyone at the party was someone I had met and become close to as a result of my job search."

QUICK TIP:

- Prepare for a long search.

- Is this the best thing that could happen?

- Manage the new freedom.

Richard Longabaugh

Notes and Ideas

Section 2
Gathering Your Tools

6) **Support Groups**
7) **Government Resources**
8) **Job Search in the**
   Electronic Age
9) **Networking**
10) **The Elevator Speech**
11) **Resume/Business Cards/**
   Cover Letters
12) **Record Keeping**
13) **Non-Job Search Activities**
14) **Job Boards**
15) **Recruiters**

5. Support Groups

More truth: job search should NEVER be a solitary activity.

Quite simply, you can't do it on your own. No matter how independent you are or how successful you have been in your career, you will not be successful on your own. The sooner you learn this truth, the quicker your search will gain traction.

There is much in the American character that celebrates the virtues of rugged individualism, go-it-alone, and self-sufficiency. When it comes to job search, that's a lot of bunk, or as a friend keeps telling me it's "a pile of the well-known brown article." Though many try, it is a rare individual indeed who finds a job without some assistance.

Getting the wisdom and counsel of others is key to a focused, mature job search. Acknowledging your need for, and accepting, the help of others is an essential recovery step in making the transition from a wounded ex-employee with arrows in your back to a successful job seeker.

Caution: As noted earlier, be careful how much you rely on your spouse or family for support. Unless they have been unemployed, it is not fair to expect them to understand what you are going through.

For example, you may walk in the door and be greeted by "Honey, how was your day?" You hear "Do you have a job yet?" All your spouse wanted to know was how your day was. The potential for misunderstanding and increased tension will grow unless managed. To be sure, you need to keep you family posted on search. However, try to keep the information flow at the macro level and spare your loved ones the gritty and emotional details of your search.

Where do you turn to share your frustrations and blow off that harmful search steam? Your best source of support comes from people who are having a similar experience. Trust me on this one.

NETWORKING GROUPS

Early in your new jobless state, find and join at least one job networking group.

What are job networking groups? Sometimes thought of as "AA for the Unemployed" (no disrespect intended) typically, these are groups of fellow seekers who meet to share experiences, leads, and horror stories, or offer job search tips. They may be sponsored by a government agency, a non-profit organization, or a church.

I am a major supporter of faith-based initiatives. Some of these church groups spring up as well-intended support efforts for unemployed members of the congregation. Prayer and sympathy abound. However, these groups often fail when the founder gets a job or it becomes apparent to the members that more than polite words are needed to find a job.

Networking groups are as varied as their organizers and often are free or have minimal fees. Some follow a curriculum while others may focus on speakers or developing particular skills. Each group will adopt customs and rituals that make it unique. The important thing is to find a group that suits you and attend regularly.

Do some personal due diligence. Check to see how long the group has been meeting, who runs the meetings, if specific searching skills are taught, and how many graduates there are from the program.

Look for job support group resources in your local area. They may be attached to a church or a library, called a Job Club or other names, or be known to your state unemployment department. Connections like this are an invaluable aid when it comes to helping job seekers connect to networking groups and other resources.

Spending all your time attending seminars or networking meetings is not going to get you a job. These should be used as information-gathering and support opportunities. They are not a substitute for your own work.

> **Caution:**
> **Do not confuse activity with results.**

ACCOUNTABILITY GROUPS

I have made several references to accountability groups. An accountability group is different from a networking group in several ways. Typically, these are much smaller gatherings of similarly minded folks—fewer than six members seem to work best. You may hear some seekers refer to these groups as their personal board of directors.

These groups are independent of networking groups although may have emerged from seekers who are in a networking group. The focus is to support each other in their search and hold members accountable for making demonstrable progress.

If you tell your group that you are going to have four informational interviews next week, you are expected to report honestly on your results at the next meeting. Should you fall short, you can expect a hard, but supportive, challenge from the others in the group. These groups are characterized by absolute candor, metrics, follow-through, and commitment to results. Clearly, this is not for everyone but if you are serious, find a group. Better yet, start your own! Accountability groups can make the journey easier because you are traveling with like-minded seekers.

JOB COACHES

If you are uncomfortable in a group setting or feel the need for individual attention, finding a job coach can be highly beneficial. There is a distinction to be made here. We are not talking about psychological counseling or therapy. Determining the need and value of those services is beyond the scope of this book. Coaches, on the other hand, are in the business of advising you on strategies that lead to a successful job search.

There are many qualified individuals who, through formal training or experience, counsel individuals in job search. In searching for a coach, don't be dazzled by certifications or extra initials after their name. This is an endeavor where experience and track record are more important than formal training. Seek the advice and recommendation of others who have been in the job search game to help you find a coach.

Job coaches can help with tasks ranging from resume preparation to interview coaching. Advice from these pros can be helpful in providing perspective on a job seeker's skills or suggesting guidance on career-pathing. Just remember, if you go the coach/counselor route, be prepared to pay their fee.

Many coaches or advisers earn their living or promote their practice by giving seminars or speeches. These can provide good insights to the search process and keep you in touch with current practices or technology. Speakers can be inspiring or help get you back on track if you are on the downward slide of the roller-coaster. However, no coach, speaker, (or certainly this author), has the silver bullet or secret formula for finding a job. There is just no substitute for the heavy lifting job seekers need to do on their own behalf.

QUICK TIPS:
- Don't try this alone.
- Join networking groups.
- Coaches can help.
- You need to do the work.

Notes and Ideas

6. Government Resources

Ditch your prejudices and preconceived notions about government programs or the people they are intended to help.

Regardless what you think of "the government," this is one area not to be ignored by the job seeker. Yes, there are many conspicuous examples of wasteful, bureaucratic programs that are supposed to be consumer-friendly (welfare, DMV, health care, the VA) but employment and job creation programs are a politician's favorite deliverable, typically making them well-funded and attractive resources.

Admittedly, the quality of the services received will vary depending on the person behind the desk or the specific location, but these offices are a wealth of good information and often promote themselves as one-stop shopping. You may encounter crowded resource rooms or long waits for some services but learn how to avoid those peak periods.

States sponsor extensive listings of job openings, usually electronically, seminars on a plethora of relevant topics, access to computer labs, services of job counselors, tips on interviewing (sometimes video interviewing), numerous publications, and search advice.

The federal government is awash in information that can be useful to your search. In addition to its own extensive job listings, salary ranges, labor statistics, job titles, and position descriptions, check to see if there are industry-specific programs or initiatives to help displaced workers with retraining. Similarly, each state will have its own variety of programs for the unemployed. (See Appendix 2.)

You may be compelled to use government services if, for example, you receive unemployment compensation. Weekly registration is often mandatory to receive payments. Even if you are not required to register, it is often in your best interest to become familiar with state services.

Don't neglect colleges and universities. As an alum, you may be entitled to use your alma mater's career services. Also, be aware of extension services and other programs housed within a university setting that may be directed at career advancement, certifications and job coaching.

In any case, it's up to you to do some serious research into the scores of government programs. This is a research source greater than you can imagine and for the most part, it's free!

QUICK TIPS:

- Get over your pre-conceived notions.

- Prepare to be overwhelmed.

Notes and Ideas

7. Job Search in the
Electronic Age

W hen was the last time you looked for a job? If it has been more than five years, you are out of touch.

Life in the electronic age has dramatically changed the way people find jobs. If you've been living on a deserted island or just gotten electricity in your cave and it's been 10 years since you did a job search, yes, Monster.com still exists. If your time frame is even longer, you can take comfort in the fact that you can still find employment ads, even though the newspaper you used to read may no longer be published.

The single best electronic tool in your job search toolbox is LinkedIn. It is likely that LinkedIn has been instrumental in more than half of all successful job searches since 2010. Some reports put that number closer to 80 percent. For the uninitiated, LinkedIn is the adult, professional version of Facebook.

For all the importance this book places on LinkedIn, the reader will find few references to the tool. The reason is quite simple. This book will not be able to keep pace with the changes in technology nor can it do justice to the topic. There are a number of excellent books, tutorials, and seminars that do a far better treatment of LinkedIn than we can do here. LinkedIn gurus exist in every community and should be sought out for their expertise in using this software for job search. Quite frankly, my two favorites are a pair of Wisconsinites: Wayne Breitbarth (1) and Sue Gresham (2).

The Internet has spawned hundreds of resources to help the job seekers. See the partial list in Appendix II in the back of this book. It goes without saying, but job seekers need to be Internet savvy if they are going to be successful. If you are a Baby Boomer (as opposed to a Millennial), it is essential that you overcome any fear of computers or the Internet. Sorry, you oldsters, it's just a fact.

It's not just job seekers who use the Internet. Most recruiters are very skilled at using a variety of Internet tools and begin their searches by checking resources such as LinkedIn. If you want to be found, then you need to be where they are looking. (More on recruiters in Chapter 14.)

Let me pause to comment on interviewing and the Internet. Electronic conferencing has been available for many years but only tangentially affected the interviewing process. All this changed with the pandemic scare in 2020. While many businesses hit the pause button and hiring slowed, interviewing did not stop.

Video interviewing became the norm and many candidates accepted new jobs without ever having face-to-face meetings with their new boss. Some of the old interviewing protocols have returned but job seekers need to be more flexible on company interview policies. Check Chapter 19 for tips on how to have an effective video interview.

QUICK TIPS:

- Prepare to join the electronic age.

- Consider LinkedIn an indispensable tool.

- Internet, Internet, Internet.

RESOURCES:

(1) Wayne Breitbarth, *The Power Formula for LinkedIn Success*, Fourth Edition, Greenleaf, 2019.

(2) Sue Gresham (www.sue-gresham.com)

Notes and Ideas

8. Networking

You can't do it alone. I said this back in Chapter 5. Now do yourself a favor and take it to heart.

The answer is networking. Ads, recruiters, and job boards can be important, but even when all these resources are considered, networking is how most people find their jobs.

To be sure, networking can be the scariest and most rewarding part of job search.

What makes networking so scary? Unless you do this for a living, as would someone in sales, most of us view it right up there with public speaking—a horror to be avoided. I'll talk later about how to overcome some of those fears.

What makes networking the most rewarding part of job search? First, it is the path to a successful search, and second, the amazing collection of people you are about to meet.

The phrase, "It's not *what* you know but *who* you know" used to have an unmistakable stink to it. Tainted with an old-world sense of elitism, the implication seemed to be that your talents and skills weren't as important as who your daddy knew. Realizing that you are now well into the 21st century, it's time to wake up to reality.

Let's define the term. Networking is nothing more than being connected to anyone who can help you in your job search. Seekers may find Joe Sweeney's book, *Networking Is a Contact Sport*, (1) a useful read.

You probably have a bigger network than you realize but you need to manage it, grow it, and work it. Networking in the electronic age has a great friend called LinkedIn. However, this is not a task to be left to the Internet and hoping job prospects will magically appear.

Who should be in your network? Anyone you knew, know, or will meet who might be able to help you.

Start with professional contacts and coworkers like those people you didn't disparage when you got *The Boot*. Don't forget colleagues from past jobs and employers, even those from ten or more years ago. I know of several successful searches that came through leads from fellow employees as far back as 20 years ago. These are all people who know and like you and can speak to your career successes.

Did you go to school? Of course, you did. Classmates from high school, college, fraternities, sororities, training programs, and grad school are logical networking contacts. Who do you know or have met through trade associations or industry groups? What about neighbors, the retired widow across the alley, clubs, volunteer groups, religious affiliations, sports teams?

Okay, you get the idea, but that widow? The point is you don't know who she knows, like her son who is the VP of Marketing at a major big box retailer.

When you were employed, did you belong to any trade associations or professional groups? Were you expected to resign from those when you got *The Boot*? Don't quit just because your former employer is no longer paying the dues. These are your peers and professional colleagues who represent some of the best networking connections you could have. Contact the association and explain your new job status. Its goal is to maintain healthy membership numbers and you may find that it will allow a dues-free (or low-cost) membership until you land a new job.

> **Caution:**
> **Numbers alone do not make a great network. Be discerning about who you include. These are not your Christmas card or Facebook Friends lists.**

My assumption is that you will manage your network on your computer and through LinkedIn. A spreadsheet or yellow legal pad just will not do the trick as you may be accessing your network multiple times a day.

Did you take your Rolodex, customer list, or company roster with you before you got *The Boot*? Be careful. This information may be construed as company property and your possession of it may put you at some risk.

Work your network by refreshing your connections regularly—about every six weeks. Most people have short memories and will need to be reminded that you are in a job search. A brief update or cleverly worded "hello" will do.

QUICK TIPS:

- Network, network, network.

- Built it, grow it, work it.

- Be deliberate but careful.

RESOURCES:

(1) Joe Sweeney, *Networking Is a Contact Sport*, BenBella Books (2011).

Notes and Ideas

9. The Elevator Speech

Y ou won't see that term in this book again. I hate it!
Conventional wisdom says as you get on at the ground level of an elevator, you should be able to make your case to a CEO, or someone else you don't know, in the time it takes for the elevator to get to his floor—about 30 seconds. I absolutely disagree. After many years of job coaching, I am convinced that the most important principles in job search are *brevity* and *clarity*. If you disagree with me, stop reading this book. I can't help you.

Why?

It is short-sighted and selfish to assume someone will give you 30 seconds to babble on about yourself. Think about it from the CEO's perspective. Can you listen, and pay attention, to someone who talks about themselves for 30 seconds? Very difficult. Most people have the attention span of a goldfish, so whatever you say after the first few seconds won't be remembered. This also assumes you manage to overcome the person's irritation at being assaulted by a desperate job seeker. Good luck.

There is a nasty trick I play when leading a group of job seekers. I ask the attendees to introduce themselves to the group. Invariably, the first respondent will try to cram as much personal information as possible into the next minute in an effort to impress the group. At some point, I will unceremoniously cut him off, clutching my throat and making a gagging sound. Cruel, but here's the point.

I'll then ask the group what they remember. Predictably, their responses will reflect a smattering of selective hearing. This is human nature at work and counterproductive if you want someone to know about you. The longer you talk, the more people forget the opening of your monologue and your message gets fuzzy. Is that really the impression you want to leave? Hardly. It is your responsibility to correct that.

What is the answer? ***Brevity***. I limit introductions to 10 words or less. "Impossible," most people say and yet, with some practice, everyone can do it.

Imagine yourself at the next networking event, cocktail party, or neighborhood barbeque. Someone will ask you, "What do you do?" Even in the most casual situations, no one wants to listen to you talk about yourself for the next 30 seconds.

The goal in an initial exchange with someone is to start a conversation. This same principle applies to a casual neighborhood meeting, an encounter at the bar, or an interview.

What's the secret? In your 10-word introduction, give the other person a reason to ask you a question.

Once your listener asks a question, you know what's on his mind and can speak accordingly. If you start talking about your job search and all they want to know is a recommendation for a good burger joint, the potential for an unfulfilling exchange goes up exponentially. Be patient and let things flow naturally. Talk about the burger joint because you want to move past the introduction and get to know the other person. Show a genuine interest in what he or she has to say. If the conversation goes well, you may be able to work it into a job search discussion. If not, enjoy the event but make plans to meet again later.

Here are some examples of memorable 10-word introductions. Think about the questions and conversation that would follow. Study them as you create your own 10-word masterpiece.

- "I ship the impossible."

- "I'm the Swiss army knife of mechanical engineers."

- "I help consumers make good buying decisions."

- "I bake and my desserts make the main course forgettable."

- "I make my boss look good."

You will be amazed at the kind of conversation that follows a brief, yet clear, introduction.

Notice the lack of fluff in the above introductions. The economy of words is important here. ***Clarity.*** Choose words that have an impact and you will find the Internet is full of suggestions. However, don't go overboard trying to sound smart or like someone you are not. If humor is not your true nature, don't try to be funny. You need to learn to read your audience and modify your introduction appropriately. For example, don't use industry jargon at a neighbor's barbeque. Do not waste words.

My pet peeve is when seekers say they are "experienced" or "professional." Someone should be able to discern those things about you without your having to tell them. Banish those words from your vocabulary.

One last thought: people hire people they like. Your likeability goes up when you have a conversation. In a series of studies in 2017, psychologist Karen Huang and her colleagues discovered that "people who ask more questions, particularly follow-up questions, are better liked by their conversation partners."

In other words, the person who speaks the most in a conversation usually has a more positive assessment of the conversation and by extension, the other person. A positive impression of the conversation is exactly what you want to leave with the other party.

In other words, you should be the one asking the questions. Keep that in mind before you start to prattle on about your accomplishments. Don't worry—you'll get your chance to shine.

QUICK TIPS:

- Use fewer than 10 words.

- Say something clever or funny, but only if it comes naturally.

- Avoid biz-speak and corporate jargon.

- Choose words carefully for impact.

- Don't say you are "experienced" or "professional."

RESOURCES:

(1) Joe Keohane, "How to Become a Master at Talking to Strangers," *Entrepreneur Magazine*, July 2021.

10. Resumes/ Business Cards/ Cover Letters

RESUMES

Give your resume to ten people for their comments and you'll get a dozen replies.

Yes, the disconnect is on purpose. Said another way, there are lots of opinions on what constitutes a good resume. I don't spend a lot of time on this topic because there are plenty of "experts" who make a living rewriting resumes. There are also many books written on the subject and this isn't one of them. That's not to say "do whatever feels good," so here are some generally accepted themes on how you should prepare your resume.

The top third of your resume is the most important. This part of your resume will get about two seconds (literally) of attention from a hiring manager. If your format is not crisp, your type font too small, there are too many words, or not enough key words (see below), it's off to the circular file.

If the reader is captivated, make sure she only has two pages to read and that your resume relates as closely as possible to the position description. Use bullets and specific accomplishments. Quantitative information expressed as a number, such as percent sales increase or dollars saved, add depth but don't overuse. The current thinking is that you only need to go back 10 to 15 years in your career.

It almost goes without saying that the best way to kill your candidacy is to lie, fabricate, or grossly inflate your accomplishments on your resume. For many years, Milwaukee recruiter Jude Werra compiled a Liars' Index. At one point, he calculated that as many as one of every six candidates committed resume fraud by falsifying credentials, primarily in the area of education. Don't do it!

How many resumes should you have? This is a trick question because you need a new one for every application you make. Don't faint. Start with a master resume and customize it for each job. The how and why are critical to your success and revolve around the use of *keywords*.

Many companies make use of automated resume readers to deal with the hundreds of applicants that may result from posting a position on job sites. These software programs are written to screen candidates based on the number of words in the resume that match those in the position profile. These are the keywords. The higher the number of matching words, the greater likelihood the candidate will make it through the initial screening. Even if a human is doing the initial screening, he or she is looking for certain words on the resume.

Keywords come from the published position descriptions. Your task is to incorporate as many of these keywords as possible on your resume. This is what is meant by having a new resume for each application. The essential elements and format of your resume will not change significantly. However, the emphasis might, based on your use of keywords.

> **Caution:**
> **The resume is just a tool and not the silver bullet in your job search.**

Many job seekers place too much emphasis on their resume. Yes, it should be readable and honest, but a resume's job is to get you a contact or call. Too many seekers spend way too much time creating the "perfect" resume in the mistaken belief that's what job search is all about.

BUSINESS CARDS

You need them. Get them. Almost any commercial printer or business supply retailers can handle business cards, including on-line printers such as Vista-Print. Many home computers have software programs that can print business cards if you get business card stock.

Don't invest time or money on an elegant production. Unless you are looking for a graphic arts position, most readers don't really care. It's an information piece. Avoid muted colors or elaborate floral designs as they make it hard on the reader, particularly in low light.

The most important features on a business card are your name and how you can be contacted. The type font on your name should be larger than other information. After all, your name is the reason for the card. Under your name, you can list a job function or title such as: Mechanical Engineer," "Business Analyst," "Teacher," "Non-Profit Executive," "Customer Service Manager," "Software Engineer," "Account Manager," and so on.

If you are concerned about privacy issues, don't include a street address. However, your e-mail address and phone numbers are essential. If you have more than one phone number, identify which is your cell phone as some employers may contact you via text messages. Please do not use a micro-font for your phone number or email. It's really irritating when someone has to drag out reading glasses to read your phone number. Make it bigger.

A side note about e-mail. If you have a cute email address, drop it. "YOURNAME@Buffboy.com" or "YOURNAME@Mommydearest.com" are not as flattering as you think and undermine your professional credibility. Gmail is popular among many seekers.

Consider using the back of your business card. This is a convenient place to list some of your accomplishments, job skills, StrengthsFinder, or desired titles.

Cover Letters

Love 'em or hate 'em. Opinions among recruiters and hiring managers are divided on the subject. Some view a cover letter as an essential part of your application while others (like me) never read them. If read, the cover letter can highlight aspects of your resume that are germane to the position, offer explanation of job changes or provide other information of interest to the reader. On the other hand, it if does not get read, who cares what you said?

How do you know if a cover letter is appropriate? A careful reading of the position description often provides the best clues. If one is requested, send it. If still uncertain, contact the recruiter, HR-Heather (our mythical, ubiquitous HR person), or the hiring manager to determine their expectations. When in doubt, go ahead and write a short one but make sure it is not done in haste. You don't want poor grammar or misspellings to leave a fatal impression.

Quick Tips:

- Make your resume readable.

- Make your business cards readable.

- Make your email address professional.

- Proofread everything (at least) twice.

Notes and Ideas

11. Record Keeping

As discussed in Chapter 4, one of the challenges you will need to address is how you manage your time. For better or worse, your job dictated how and where you spent your time. With that constraint now gone, it's now up to you to optimize the hours in your day.

Conventional (uninformed) opinion says that your old job took 40+ hours of your week so you should spend the same amount of time on your search. NO! Job search is hard work and you cannot expect to work eight hours a day or 40 hours a week. You will burn out long before you get a job. (See Chapter 12.)

However, how you spend your time is important. Not every task is of equal weight or importance and the particular activities will change as your search matures. As noted in Chapter 4, the best way to know where and how you spent your time is to maintain a log or timesheet noting the task and how much time it took. Review your log each week and evaluate your priorities.

Early in your search, develop the habit of chronicling your journey in a diary or journal. Keep notes on who you met, the nature of your conversation, follow-up dates, referrals, leads, applications, and so on. You are going to quickly accumulate more information than your head can absorb so this notebook will be an important resource for you. Notes on a computer may work for you but a three-ring binder with subject tabs is tough to beat.

QUICK TIP:
- You are only as efficient as the records you keep.

Notes and Ideas

12. Non-Job Search Activities

At some time in your search, an interviewer, family member, or friend is likely to ask, "So, what have you been doing since you lost your job?"

Not only is this a legitimate question, but a great opportunity. Your answer should obviously include a brief description of your commitment to a comprehensive job search, but there are a number of other activities that could be included in your answer. My not-so-subtle suggestion here is that you should consider doing some, or all, of the following.

Earlier, I disagreed with the sentiment that you should be committing 40 hours a week to your search. After all, your job should be to find a job. True, but search is exhausting and people who have never been unemployed will not understand this circumstance.

To keep yourself fresh, mentally alert, and interview ready, you need to strike a balance between job search and other activities. My job search colleagues recommend you spend not more than 30 hours per week on your search. I agree.

EDUCATION

As a consequence of your unemployment, an employer wants to know that you have not lost your skills or professional edge. This is particularly true in fast-paced industries or disciplines such as information technology. Take classes or Internet courses that keep you current in your industry. Picking up a certification or pursuing a degree shows you are not only a life-long learner, but that you have stayed in touch with recent trends and best practices.

> **Secret Tip:**
> **You don't need to have completed the course. It is often sufficient just to be able to say you are actively pursuing a degree or certificate program.**

VOLUNTEER

If you are not already involved in community, religious, or other non-profit activities, jump in. You have the time and your experience will be welcome. Volunteering gets you out of the house, away from the computer and interacting face to face with live people. Job search is often a solitary, focused journey. Volunteering affords the opportunity to meet people without the pressures of your search. Think of it as a mental health vacation. Volunteering, particularly for those looking to work in a non-profit or mission-driven enterprise, can also be a way to introduce yourself to a potential employer.

FAMILY

Research has shown that more than 20 percent of job seekers found their time of unemployment coincided with the need to attend to personal or family medical issues. Whether you took care of a long-ignored personal medical problem or were a caregiver to a family member, this is a reality for "sandwich generation" workers who have children living in their basement and aging parents in their guest room.

This is a legitimate answer to the question, and you should not feel guilty or shy about divulging the fact. However, you should NOT feel pressured to discuss any medical details in an interview. All you need to do is assure the interviewer that the issue has been resolved and will not affect your availability for work.

HEALTH

If you are not physically active, commit to some personal health goals, such as weight loss. If running a marathon is on your bucket list, get started. There are tons of scientific data to support the claim that people live longer, sleep better, and are more mentally alert when physically active. Fair or not, it is a reality that most hiring managers are more inclined to favor candidates who present themselves as physically fit vs. those who are overweight and flabby.

Note:
Job search can be highly stressful, if not depressing. Don't neglect your mental health. However, this is not an appropriate topic to bring up in an interview.

Do those things necessary to keep yourself mentally healthy: hang around happy, positive people; renew your spiritual life; share your honest emotions with trusted colleagues. Carrying a good attitude into an interview starts with your mental wellness.

Part-time Work

Whether you call yourself a consultant or part-time employee, this is an excellent answer to this chapter's question. Some job seekers say that they can't look for a new job and hold down a part-time or contract assignment. Nonsense. Economic necessity often demands that job seekers take a position that is not full time or even in their desired field. Part-time work is particularly appropriate for someone who is facing long-term job loss. The goal is not only to generate an income, but to stay engaged in a commercial activity.

One advantage to being a part-timer is that it keeps you active in the industry. Among some employers, a trend becoming popular is the use of temp-to-perm assignments. The employer offers a candidate a position that is identified up front as temporary or short-term. This arrangement may be driven by an employer's financial uncertainty or a try-it-before-you-buy-it philosophy, but it also gives the employee a foot in the door if an opportunity becomes available for permanent, full-time position.

Some seekers worry that taking a part-time position or side job will be viewed skeptically by employers. This is not necessarily true as the business world gets used to the "gig economy." Turning a hobby or other unpaid vocation into a paying proposition shows creativity and the entrepreneurial spirit prized by many employers.

> **Note:**
> *I have seen several cases where a job seeker has turned the gig job into a permanent position. Perhaps losing your job wasn't so bad after all.*

QUICK TIPS:

- Don't let the job search crush you.

- Get off the computer.

- Can you turn a side hustle into a career?

Notes and Ideas

13. Job Boards

Job boards get a bad rap from seekers, counselors, and me. The fact is, however, there is no greater concentration of jobs than those posted on various Internet sites. At one time, job boards like Monster.com were the vanguard of modern job search.

These days, almost everyone who has a job to fill will post it electronically somewhere. Company websites, Internet job boards, government agencies, and recruiters are among the most prolific posters of employment openings. Low cost, maximum views and massive distribution are some of the reasons for them to go this route.

Clearly, job boards should not be ignored or discounted as they represent one of several paths that might lead to employment. The challenge, however, is to understand their limitations and not become addicted to them. Check Appendix 2 to see a partial listing of job boards.

I wish I could tell you this is an excellent use of your time. I can't because it is not. If you are keeping an honest log of your time (See Chapter 4), at the end of the week, you will be stunned at how much time you spent looking at job boards.

> **Caution:**
> **Job boards can be seductive.**

It is all too easy to start your job search day by checking job postings on your favorite job board. Then you check other sites and more after that. Pretty soon, you've blown past lunch and you start to think you've had a productive day.

It is important to make a distinction here between trolling the Internet for jobs and other computer work. You need computer time to respond to emails, set up interviews, contact your network, and other essential duties. The trap rookie job seekers fall into is believing that time spent on job boards equals quality job search time. Yes, the job boards can lead to a job but compared to other activities like building your network or doing informational interviews (See Chapter 19), the payoff is surprisingly poor. If you spend more than one hour a day checking out job boards, you need a reality check.

There is a caveat I need to acknowledge. To get unemployment compensation (UC) in some states, you need to demonstrate that you are actively searching for employment and not just collecting free money. One way to show search activity is to cite the number of job leads you have pursued. An easy way to generate job leads is from job boards. Just be careful not to abuse this tactic or you may lose those UC benefits.

Job boards are often a source of great frustration to seekers. Postings can easily generate hundreds of responses for an employer. Depending on the company, they respond to only a handful of the resumes and the rest go into a black hole, never to be touched again. Seekers then spend countless hours waiting for a reply to their carefully crafted, keyword-loaded resume that never comes. Investing too much time and energy on job boards will quickly put you on the down slide of the roller coaster and end in frustration.

QUICK TIPS:

- Job boards can help.

- Keep track of your time.

- Learn to manage frustration.

Notes and Ideas

14. Recruiters

The first, and last, principle in working with recruiters is: *RECRUITERS DO NOT WORK FOR YOU.*

Recruiters can be useful, but are not essential in finding a new job. It is important, however, to understand how they work and their limitations. Unless you are signing a check with the recruiter's name on it, do not forget this critical fact—the recruiter works for a company or organization that pays them to find candidates for specific positions. It is also important to understand the different kinds of recruiters.

There are three basic types of recruiters. The first is a recruiter who is an employee of the company. Typically, he or she is part of the HR team in larger companies (perhaps someone named Heather) whose job is to find candidates for a specific position within the company. Such recruiters may have a single assignment but is not unusual for a company recruiter to have a dozen or more active assignments. It's not hard to understand, therefore, why they are very busy and not likely to give you much attention or even return phone calls. Company recruiters may stay with you until you are hired or dismissed, or they may turn you over to another HR staffer once you are initially qualified by HR-Heather.

The second type of recruiter, regardless of what they might call themselves, works on a contingency basis. This recruiter is not an employee of the company but works for a third-party organization that will get paid by the client company if, and when, the candidate they present is hired. Companies may place a job order with more than one contingency firm, but only the firm whose candidate gets hired will get paid.

The third type of recruiter is a retained search recruiter. These recruiters are also not employees of the company with the job opening. Their firm is contracted by the employer to search for a specific candidate. Typically, they have an exclusive arrangement and may receive progress payments from the client company to fill the position. Often these are executive level positions and may take several months to fill.

I often hear complaints about recruiters who don't call or give the candidate much time.

Please understand, you may be the most successful salesman in your industry, but if a recruiter is looking for an electrical engineer and not a salesman, he has no reason to spend time with you because you aren't going to make any money for him.

Seekers who contact a recruiter, and not in response to a job posting, should expect only a few minutes with the recruiter. At best, you may be welcome to add your resume to their data base.

> *Caution:*
> *Do not sign any agreement that gives*
> *exclusive rights to a recruiter to represent*
> *you. Unless you are paying him or her to*
> *market you to a number of companies,*
> *this will prevent other contingency*
> *recruiters from presenting you to a*
> *company in which you might have*
> *an interest.*

The quality of recruiters is wide-ranging. Some do a very thorough job vetting you before presenting your credentials to an employer. Others expend a minimal effort hoping your resume alone will get you an interview. Most recruiters are ethical and will treat you professionally, but you are ultimately responsible for your own search.

Don't allow yourself to get caught between recruiters. Only one recruiter can present you to the company so it is important to know up front who is representing you. If it looks like two firms are going to fight over you for a fee, the company may avoid the fight and drop you as a candidate. If you have already applied to the company, tell the recruiter and he or she can deal with HR-Heather over company policies regarding recruiters.

What to do if the recruiter calls you? Be professional and don't act like this is your first rodeo.

Questions to ask a recruiter:

- Are you an employee of the company?

- What is the name of the company?

- If the name is withheld, when can I find out the company?

- Is the search confidential or is it posted on a job board?

- Do you have an exclusive arrangement with the company?

- Have you worked for this company prior to this assignment?

- What types of positions have you filled for them?

- What is your experience in this industry?

- What kind of communication can I expect from you?

- Do you prefer I communicate via email or phone with you?

- Will you be doing the compensation negotiations?

- Will you be doing the reference checks?

- Can I determine or restrict the information you share?

- Will you provide feedback after an interview?

- Will you tell me before you share my name with a client?

Dealing with recruiters can be very frustrating, but once you understand what role they play in a search, you will be better able to manage your emotions. Recruiters may be very engaging over the phone, but you are not their new best friend.

Notes and Ideas

Section 3
Interviewing

15. Interview Preface

The next section of this book is about interviewing. Don't spend time on this section and certainly don't start interviewing unless you have read and absorbed the wisdom in all the previous chapters. Interviewing is the product of a lot of preparation. Although you have reached this waypoint, there are still miles to go in this marathon.

I have identified three types of interviews:

1) informational
2) phone or virtual
3) Face-to-face

Each type is different and must be mastered. However, if you are emotionally well prepared, have taken to heart the earlier sections of this book, and have done your homework, you have little to fear.

Interview experiences are cumulative, and your first interviews are just not going to be as good as later ones. In other words, don't interview for your dream job right out of the gate. Use your early interviews to hone your skills for the jobs you really want.

In this section, I have also selected four examples of questions you are likely to face. You may be disappointed not to find more detailed advice on how to handle interview questions. In truth, you should be able to anticipate about 80 percent of the questions that might be asked and can prepare for those on your own. When in doubt, ask your accountability group or networking meeting to critique your proposed answers. Once you get comfortable with how you might respond to a particular question, write it down and then practice, practice, practice.

The four questions I've selected are the product of hundreds of job-seeker experiences and can be the most confounding. They are also questions that, if answered thoughtfully, can be the most impactful during your interview. It almost goes without saying but, if you stumble or try to wing it on any one of these four, you could blow the interview.

You should get used to the idea right now that not every interview is going to be a winner and that's okay. Controlling your emotions is a recurring theme in this book and when it comes to interviewing, the more relaxed, the better. Author Natalie Fischer, in *8 Mind Tricks That Will Set You Up for Interview Success*, (1) recommends that you not be attached to the outcome of an interview. The concern is that if your interview expectations are too high, anything less will be disappointing. Keep in mind, too, that unlike your old calculus class, you don't need to have a perfect interview for it to be successful. This is a human endeavor and humans are not perfect.

If you are ready, let's read on.

RESOURCES:

(1) Natalie Fischer, *8 Mind Tricks That Will Set You Up for Interview Success*, Firsthand, 3/29/2021.

Notes and Ideas

_____

_____

_____

_____

_____

_____

_____

_____

_____

_____

_____

_____

_____

_____

_____

_____

_____

_____

16. Your Appearance and Behavior

Sociologists report that when people meet, impressions are formed in less than two seconds, 75 percent of which are non-verbal. This means the interviewer will spend the rest of your meeting either confirming or refuting her initial impressions. In other words, a good first impression is just as hard to overcome as a bad first impression, so make it easy on yourself.

Look no further than your mother for tips on making a good first impression. What did she tell you? Comb your hair. Stand up straight. Look the other person in the eye. Use a firm handshake. Remember names. Shine your shoes. Dress nicely. The echoes of her often-unwelcome advice are now fundamental. Do it. Follow those admonitions. They make a difference.

Clean-shaven faces or neatly trimmed beards are acceptable but make sure, men and women, that your hair is combed and you are not a victim of the wind-blown look. The wet look is a turn-off. Leave your personal fashion statement at home. Cover tattoos and bare shoulders.

We should also mention here that you need to arrive early for your interview. In doing so, be careful regarding your parking lot behavior. Your arrival has been anticipated by your interviewer and parking lot watching is a favorite sport of some employees. Don't complete your toilet in the car or spit out mouthwash in the parking lot. You never know who is watching. NO smoking in the car. Your clothes will reek of smoke and it can be very offensive.

Perfume or aftershave should be left at home in the original sealed container. No matter how marvelous you feel about your favorite fragrance, don't abuse the olfactory senses of the interviewer or interview panel. As your prospective colleagues, they may not welcome the prospect of your scent floating over the cubicle next to them. This can be a real turn-off in an interview.

What to wear? Give some thought to this topic. If it has been a few years since you updated your wardrobe or you've gotten used to yoga pants in your home office, get some fashion advice—maybe from your kids. You don't want to look frumpy or wear out-of-date fashions. Guys often ask if they should wear a suit and tie. Most recruiters advise "yes." It is not a sin to overdress, so at a minimum, wear a sports coat and tie. You can always take the tie off, but you don't want to be the only one in the room without one.

When in doubt about your attire, ask the interviewer or hiring manager. If you wear a suit in a blue-jeans workplace, it may signal that you didn't care enough to check out the company's culture in advance and thus may not fit in.

Once, I saw a bumper sticker on a police car that said, "Attitude is Everything." The same can be said about job search. All other things in a candidate being equal, people tend to hire people they like. So, be likeable. This sounds a little glib, but your attitude will go a long way toward a successful search. No one wants to be around, let alone hire, a Debbie Downer or Glass-Half-Empty George. Be positive, upbeat, and cheerful (even in the face of a second or third rejection).

Psychologists will tell you that we remember negative events and people longer than we do most good things. The goal is to be memorable for your accomplishments and not for the wrong things like a poor attitude. I recommend you read *Attitude Is Everything* by Keith Harrell. (1) This is a terrific read and a good way to get you in the right frame of mind.

Finally, remember the "little people." With all due respect, we mean receptionists, secretaries, and assistants. Your first good impression should be made with them. It is not unusual for the hiring manager to circle back to a receptionist to get their impression of a candidate. If you can't be friendly and engaging with a company's front-line employee, how will you behave with a client?

QUICK TIPS:

- Remember your mother's advice.
- Dress for success.

RESOURCES:

(1) *Attitude Is Everything* by Keith Harrell, Harper Collins Publishers, 2005 edition.

Notes and Ideas

17. Interview Preparation

B e a Boy Scout or a Girl Scout. The Scout motto: "Be Prepared."

Congratulations! You've gotten to the point in your search where you are being invited for interviews. Good news, but now the real work begins.

Below are a number of hints on interviewing. Admittedly, they are somewhat random. Subsequent chapters will deal with some specific interview types and questions. You should expect some good and some not-so-good interviews but they will get better with experience.

Don't be a wimp. All too often, job seekers go into an interview feeling like they are "damaged goods." (Re-read Chapter 2) This can leave the impression you lack confidence in your own abilities. It is reasonable to be a bit nervous in your first few interviews but learn how to manage your emotions. Unemployment is a circumstance, not a permanent status. So, suck it up, Buttercup, and learn how to present the best version of you.

Do not think of an interview as an inquisition. If that's how you go into every interview, change your attitude. A good interview is not just question, answer, next question. Yes, you may get such an interview, particularly if you are talking with HR-Heather (see Chapter 19). However, in the case of the hiring manager, the best interviews are conversations. The more you can get him to talk, the better. You can ask questions about the company, the position, or the interviewer himself. These are all topics on which he is the expert and more inclined to open up.

How do you get smart about the company or the hiring manager? Preparation. Research the company through their annual report, trade publications, websites, and other Internet sources. Research the hiring official and anyone else you are scheduled to meet via company information and the internet. This is a great use of LinkedIn.

ILLEGAL QUESTIONS

One area where HR-Heather is likely to be more knowledgeable than the hiring manager is when it comes to asking illegal questions. The Equal Employment Opportunity Act (EEO) prohibits an employer or potential employer from asking questions that might even have the appearance of discrimination. Off-limit topics include:

- Age

- Race / Color

- Ethnicity

- Gender

- Sex

- Sexual orientation or gender identity

- Country of origin

- Birthplace

- Religion

- Disability

- Marital status

- Family status

- Pregnancy

- Salary history (in some states)

It can be easy to slip into these areas as familiarity increases between candidate and interviewer. Some people say that if you, as a candidate, bring up any of those topics, they are fair game. I'm not so sure. My advice is to stay alert and just don't go there.

Caution.
Your interviewer may not know
how to interview.

Once you get past the HR folks whose job it is to do interviews, don't be surprised if the hiring manager is a lousy interviewer. Often this is because that's not what he or she does regularly and might be as nervous as you. Make it easy on the hiring manager and remember, the goal is to have a conversation.

If you have prepared properly, you can probably anticipate most of the questions an interviewer will ask. Preparation and knowledge are fundamental, but technique is essential. If you are uncertain about your public speaking skills, Toastmasters International is a great organization to join.

POINTERS:

- **Brevity.** Keep your answers short and in direct response to the question. If the interview wants to know more, she'll ask.

- **Clarity.** Write your answers to likely questions in advance of any interview and practice with a friend. Use impactful words, avoid jargon and biz-speak.

- **Avoid the tendency to ramble.** Diarrhea of the mouth can be fatal.

- Every once in a while, **pause before answering a question.** A pause gives the impression of a thoughtful (not rehearsed) response.

- Practice avoiding "umms" and "ahs." Use pauses instead.

- Silence can be painful but it is better than babble. Don't feel obliged to fill every second with talk.

- Be sure you **understand the question.** It's okay to rephrase it or ask for a clarification.

- Don't fall into the trap of answering a question the interviewer did not ask. It says your listening skills are not up to par.

- **Taking an occasional note** is usually fine but don't spend the entire interview writing. You can always ask the interviewer if this is okay.

- Sit on the edge of your chair. Look enthused. Smile. Keep eye contact.

- Know the **illegal questions** in your state and prepare to deal with them.

Know your resume. As strange as this may sound, candidates often don't remember such things as the dates of previous employment or the key points under each employer. Don't let your lack of preparation create confusion in the conversation. Also, keep in mind there is a good chance the hiring manager may not have read your resume before the interview.

Know the position description (PD), or at least the one that was published. Don't let this be a speed bump on the interview road; be sure to ask at the beginning of the interview if there are any changes to the position. Don't be surprised if you are told that some things have changed since it was written. This is not a bait-and-switch tactic. It might be an old position description or a case of HR-Heather not being on the same page as the hiring manager. Sometimes the position description changes on the fly. This can happen because as the hiring manger interviews live candidates, she may discover that some attributes are more or less important than originally considered and modify the PD accordingly.

Before going any further, we should talk about rejection. Get used to it. Not that you have to like it or expect it, but in reality, very few seekers get a job after the first interview. To be sure, being turned down is a bummer but you need to gird yourself for the possibility and learn how to react. You may be told "We've decided to move in another direction" or "We've hired an internal candidate." Unfortunately, that may be all you learn. While you would like to know where you fell short, most companies instruct their HR staff to give no details for fear of lawsuits. The best advice is to swallow hard, send a polite thank-you note, and move on. I realize that's not very comforting but you now must focus on the next opportunity in your pipeline.

QUICK TIPS:

- Be a Boy Scout / Girl Scout.

- Make the interviewer comfortable.

- Know your resume.

Notes and Ideas

18. Informational Interviews

Channel your inner Barbara Walters or favorite reporter.

This is the first of our three major types of interviews. In various places throughout this book, we have emphasized the need for preparation. This includes any research you can conduct on the company or the individuals you meet. One method for gathering such intelligence is the *informational interview,* which differs significantly from either the phone/virtual or in-person interview.

Unlike other interview forms, the informational interview is not about you. It is just what the name suggests—an exercise in information gathering. Let's say there is a company, a career path, an individual, or a type of position that interests you. One of the best ways to gather such insights is to interview someone in that company or position.

Your goal is to learn as much as you can in a short amount of time. Prepare your questions in advance and don't try to wing it unless you are familiar playing the interviewer. Here's how to proceed:

1) Call or e-mail the person you would like to interview and ask for 20 minutes, perhaps over a cup of coffee. Let the person know you would like to get his or her insights on topic X. A light touch of flattery is appropriate, but don't lay it on too thick.

2) Arrive, call, or log in on time with notepad in hand. Respect the person's time and do your part to keep on schedule.

3) Remember, you are there to interview them, not the other way around. The person you're interviewing may ask some questions about you, but stay focused on the other person.

4) ***DO NOT take a resume!*** This tends to undermine the creditability of your visit. You can always send a resume later with a thank-you note.

5) The penultimate (second to last) question to ask is, "Do you know anyone else it would be helpful for me to speak with or meet?"

6) The last question is, "Is there anything I can do for you?" Usually, the other person will politely dismiss the offer. However, one executive I asked that question broke out his organization chart and asked if I knew anyone who might be able to fill

his half-dozen open positions. One person in my network fit a job and we made a connection. The executive has always taken my calls since that meeting.

QUICK TIPS:

- Be curious.

- This is not about you.

- ***NO RESUMES!***

19. The Phone or Virtual Interview

Smile, it's "go time."

The second major type of interview is the phone, or sometimes, virtual interview.

For the purposes of this discussion, assume you have already had a first encounter with the company, such as an e-mail or voice mail. However, this may be your first in-person interview. HR-Heather, the interviewer, or the recruiter is calling. What to do? Take a page from the Scouts again—***Be Prepared.***

Find out in advance how much time to allow for the conversation. Twenty to thirty minutes is a typical amount of time for an initial screening, as the task here is to determine if you are in or out of the candidate pool. Often, the recruiter is trying to screen you out. Fair or not, get used to it. Recruiters are dealing with large numbers of applicants and they need to get the pool to a manageable size.

Sometimes good candidates are lost because they did not impress the interviewer. That will not be you if you have prepared. If the conversation is scheduled for longer, the recruiter may have seen something in your paperwork that merits closer scrutiny. Don't get cocky. The interviewer still holds all the cards.

Most often, the caller is going to follow a script based on the position description, company policies, or input from the hiring manager. There is little you are going to be able to do to alter the flow, so just go with it. The questions are going to be more fact-based vs. behavioral, and may be pretty clinical.

Just because you are on the phone or monitor doesn't mean you can afford to be distracted or casual. Pick a quiet room and not a coffee shop. Keep the dogs and kids out of the room. Print out all the materials relevant to this position like your resume, personal profile, StrengthsFinder 2.0 results, position description, interview questions, and whatever other information you might need. Spread them out on the table. You do not want the interviewer to hear you shuffling papers or clicking on your computer. One colleague, Phil, recommends pasting them on a tri-fold story board and setting them on the desk behind the computer for quick reference.

In this interview, the caller will ask most of the questions. Don't expect that you will be able to direct much conversation, as this is all about the interviewer's agenda. Keep your answers brief and factual. Be knowledgeable about the company, the industry, the position, and your resume. Smile into the phone and let your enthusiasm show. Some experts suggest you stand so you don't slouch into your chairs and lose your edge.

Even though you will have a list of questions, HR Heather is running out of time and needs to write up her report. She isn't really interested in your questions and may not have the time to answer them. Therefore, prioritize your questions so you get any critical information you need.

There is one bit of data you should ask for, assuming HR-Heather hasn't already popped the question. "What is the salary for this position?" Many pros feel the person who asks first loses the advantage. I don't agree. As discussed back in Chapter 2, you need to know what your goals are and what the market is paying for the position. Don't be afraid to cite your source or industry salary data.

If your salary is in her range, say $50 to 65K, let her know your expectations are at the higher end of her range ($60 to 70K) but you are open to more conversation on the subject later (see Chapter 25). If it is not, let her know that it's not in your range but don't dwell on it. This is not the time to negotiate. She will let you know if your expectations are outside her range.

Finally, don't get trapped into giving the interviewer the amount of your last salary—it's irrelevant and can only harm you. The company has already determined the ideal salary for the position and its goal is to keep candidates within an acceptable range of that salary. Your focus needs to be on convincing the company that the value you bring to the company is compatible with its salary range. Be forward-thinking. Your old salary ties you to the past and really has no bearing on this new opportunity.

As the interview wraps up, ask if there is any more information your interviewer needs from you. If HR-Heather is satisfied, then ask the next steps and timeframe. Try to get some indication as to your status in the candidate pool—still under consideration or out? If you are out, don't whine. It probably won't do any good. She knows the candidate pool and you do not, so protesting will only irritate her.

If you are still under consideration, find out when you might expect to hear back from her or the hiring manager. You should also ask if you can follow up with any questions and via what medium—phone or email. After she hangs up, summarize the conversation in your logbook and send her a thank-you note—email is okay but handwritten is better.

Virtual or Video Interviews

A few pointers regarding virtual or video interviewing. During the era of the pandemic, most initial interviews or screenings were done via Skype, Zoom, Teams, or other Internet platform. In fact, I know of many job seekers who were hired during this time who never had a face-to-face interview or meeting with their boss even after they were hired.

Video interviewing has become a well-established means of first-round interviewing at many companies. This modality is an important cost-saving and time-saving part of an organization's interview process. This is particularly true if the position is in a distant city or means interacting with colleagues from around the country. The efficiencies are obvious, but there are some reasons for you to be concerned.

> **Caution:**
> **If you have never done a video interview or are not a user of programs like Skype, Zoom, or Teams, it is essential that you practice before your interview.**

For most of us, being recorded or filmed is not a naturally occurring activity. There's a reason TV stations hire info babes and weather geeks—they know how to act on camera. In your practice session, learn where to look, be aware of your background, check the lighting, and know how your voice and image are received. If you can do a mock video interview, review it with an eye to how you appear to others. Get an honest critique from someone other than your adoring spouse or mother.

QUICK TIPS:

- It's time to get serious.
- Understand HR-Heather's goals.
- Learn how to be a TV star.

Notes and Ideas

20. The Face-to-Face Interview

Congratulations!

You have survived HR-Heather's interview and have been invited for our third type of interview, the face-to-face interview.

If you have prepared along the way and taken to heart the advice in previous chapters, this shouldn't be as intimidating as you might think. Excitement is in the air. The most important thing to do is to relax. In fact, seasoned searchers report that their best interviews were the ones where they were so relaxed, they almost didn't care. Don't get that casual, but you get the idea.

At this point, you are emotionally and mentally ready to embrace the future. You have gotten past the anguish of losing your last job and know where you want to go. You know what to expect in the way of interview questions, your CAR stories (see Chapter 22) are well rehearsed, and you deliver your Exit Statement (see Chapter 21) like a Broadway veteran. Let the fun begin!

Every organization has a different process, so it's up to you to find out in advance what to expect. You may finally meet HR-Heather in person, have a one-on-one with the hiring manager and her boss, or possibly a panel interview with peers and subordinates.

Find out with whom you will be interviewing and for how long. Get titles and positions relative to the job for which you are interviewing. Review your research and LinkedIn data on the people you are expecting to meet. Don't be upset if the schedule changes or people are substituted in or out of the line-up. Just make sure that you get their names and business cards before you leave the building.

Panel interviews are usually awkward for everyone concerned, with each panel member having a list of specific questions to ask of all candidates. The panelists may represent a variety of reporting relationships with this position. On the other hand, some of the panelists may have been last-minute substitutions. Don't get rattled. Sit forward in your chair and be enthusiastic. Maintain good eye contact with the questioner, but glace at the other panelists to make sure they are engaged. Remember, they don't do this often and may be as nervous about this process as you. Be the calming influence in the room and try to stimulate genuine conversation.

Everyone in the hiring process may have a slightly different agenda. Your new boss, for example, wants someone who can make her look good by contributing to the team. Your peers and subordinates need comfort that you can work with the existing team and will not disrupt their norms. Your boss's boss needs to know that you can more than earn your salary by increasing revenue or controlling costs and have growth prospects for future advancement. DO NOT change your stories or alter facts presented on your resume just because you are tired of repeating yourself. The team will invariably compare notes and they should all have the same information.

If those stakeholders are happy after your interview, recruiters and hiring officials agree that the most important consideration in a new hire is fit. In other words— chemistry. What does that say about your task in an interview? Your goal is to make everyone as comfortable as possible while conveying your superior competence.

> **Caution.**
> **A lunch or dinner invitation**
> **could be your downfall.**

You may be invited to join one or more of your interviewers for a meal. While this is flattering, my advice is to decline. There are just too many things that can go wrong and many a candidacy has crashed and burned over lunch. The more relaxed, social nature of a meal can cause candidates to lose their edge.

If there is no way out of a meal, keep in mind the following:

- Do not order an alcoholic beverage even if everyone else does.

- Do not order soup or salad; these can be awkward to manage.

- Cut everything into bite-sized pieces.

- Avoid onions and garlic, which are sure to give you bad breath.

- Be consistent in your answers and do not discuss family or illegal topics.

- Remember that this is still part of the interview process.

- Be gracious and allow your host to pay the entire bill.

- Send thank-you notes, preferably hand-written, as soon as you get home.

- Record any notes or impressions in your logbook and highlight any answers could have handled better.

Now comes the hard part—waiting and patience. Before leaving, get a commitment as to when you will next hear from the company, and from whom. Do not bug HR-Heather or the hiring manager if they don't follow up as promised. You don't know why and need to resist the temptation to call or reach out.

However, after ten days of radio silence you should follow up with the hiring manager. A short, polite note reiterating your interest in the position is reasonable. Even better is to send him an article or other third-party piece about the company or industry. It shows your continued interest in a more subtle, but equally effective, manner.

Do an honest gut check. Do you really want to work here and will you be happy? If nothing else, the job-search journey is a learning process. What did you learn in this interview that will help you prepare for the next one?

QUICK TIPS:

- Read the previous chapters in this book.

- Trust your gut.

- Patience, patience, patience.

Notes and Ideas

21. The Worst Interview Question

As noted previously, when preparing for your interview, it is wise to develop answers to questions you are likely to be asked. There are numerous Internet sites with possible questions and suggested answers that can help you prepare. However, this chapter focuses on one specific question, *"What is the worst interview question you are going to face?"*

Answer: The one you don't want to be asked.

You know the question is coming and you hope HR-Heather won't ask it. You mentally twist and turn in agony fearing the worst and knowing that the success or failure of the interview can turn on how you handle this one question. Your anxiety can really make this a stressful experience.

Regardless of the specific question, preparing for this question is really quite simple: Face it head on. Name it. If you call out the demon, it becomes less scary. You have now solved half the problem.

There can be many worst interview questions but, in my experience, most job seekers dread being asked, **"How did you lose your job?"**

This is a reasonable question that HR-Heather should be expected to ask. It's just number 17 on her list of 42 she has to ask every candidate. If you answer this question successfully, it may lead to only one follow-up question and then it's on to number 18. She really isn't interested in digging up dirt unless she has reason to suspect there is a bigger story that could indicate you are a problem candidate. If she starts to drill you for more details, you'll know you blew it.

I refer to this as an ***Exit Statement***.

Solving the other half of the problem is in the preparation of your answer. There are several principles to keep in mind. Your answer should be:

- Preferably one sentence

- Honest

- Factual

- Dispassionate

In other words, DO NOT fabricate an explanation, go into detail, reinterpret the facts, bad-mouth the company, or throw the S.O.B. who fired you under the bus.

For most readers, you can take comfort in the fact that it is not about you, your job performance, or the years of loyal service you offered. There is no easier explanation than, "It's the economy, stupid."

Everyone understands the economic slowdown in 2008, or the body blow the United States suffered after 9/11, or the global pandemic. Many employers retrenched, reduced, reorganized, or refit. Millions of workers watched their jobs or companies disappear, resulting in wide-spread unemployment. Everyone knows someone who has lost their job. Quite simply, while you may be special, you are not unique when it comes to being unemployed.

Below are several examples of **Exit Statements**. Note the brevity and clarity. Really, this is all you need to say. More is not helpful.

- *"After four years in my position, the company announced a series of layoffs in response to declining revenues and my position was eliminated."*

- *"Our company lost a major contract accounting for more than 30% of our annual sales and my position was eliminated."*

- *"I survived two rounds of layoffs, but when a third round was announced, I lost my job along with seven other managers."*

Other sample responses not related to an economic downturn might be:

- *"Following a change in senior management, the company reorganized several functions and I was let go. No one was hired to replace me and I am eligible for unemployment."*

- *"Following a change in management, I received a new assignment and after a couple of months, it became clear I was not going to be contributing at a level that maximized my skills. I met with my manager and we mutually agreed I should leave the company."*

What should you say if you were terminated for cause? Own it. This may take a little more work on your part, but the principles remain the same. My experience working with Chris T. is illustrative.

Chris was a talented, self-confident manager for the airport location of a major freight carrier. We were doing an interview prep session but after an hour, we hadn't made much progress.

Something was bothering her, so I asked, "Why are you so tentative? Why are you holding back? What don't you want the interviewer to ask?"

"I got fired," she confessed. "How do I explain that?"

After some discussion, we came up with an answer. It was if the heavens had parted and the weight of the world was lifted from her shoulders. Her Exit Statement was:

- *"After 10 years with (the company), I was terminated for cause. I was trying to expedite a customer order and violated our safety policy. This was a policy that I supported and had enforced on behalf of the company. It was a painful lesson learned but I could not fault them for the decision to let me go."*

She landed a new job three weeks later.

QUICK TIPS:

- Preparation reduces stress.
- Develop an Exit Statement.
- Own it.

22. Behavioral Interview Questions

In recent years, a new type of question has become more prominent in interviews: the **behavioral interview** question. Not to be confused with the insulting "What kind of tree would you be?", this is a more sophisticated and insightful query. Typically, the question starts out "Tell me about a time when you…". There is usually no correct answer because the interviewer is looking for clues as to how you may think or act.

Behavioral interview questions can be the job seeker's best friend because they give you the chance to tell a story about your skills or accomplishments. This can be the important differentiator between you and other candidates since a well-told story makes you memorable.

While it is more challenging to prepare for behavioral interview questions, it is not impossible. There are several tried and true methodologies and they may have a variety of names such as CAR, SOAR, or STAR stories, which we will discuss shortly.

Regardless of the name, they represent a structured way to prepare your answer and seasoned seekers will typically have six to eight stories ready to go. These answers can be a little longer, two to three minutes, since you are telling a story. If you wonder where to get your stories, look at your resume and develop a story for each bullet point for your last two jobs. Team accomplishments are fine, but this is about YOU so be sure the personal pronoun "I" is prominent in your story.

The hallmarks of a CAR story, for example, are as follows:

- ***C is for Circumstance.*** As succinctly as possible, state the problem that you faced. A sentence or two should be enough. Give some background, context. Set the stage.

- ***A is for Action.*** What specific steps did you take to address the problem? Think in terms of action items. Use the personal pronoun "I." Consider adding some numbers, statistics or percentages to add depth but don't go overboard.

- ***R is for Result.*** Good or bad, what happened? Describe the result. Numbers and percentages help paint the picture. Make sure you end on a positive note. If the goal was not achieved, tell what you learned.

Sample CAR story:

- **C:** *"I was working as a product engineer in a high-volume plastics manufacturer when the plant manager said our best customer, a pharmaceutical manufacturer, was coming in to the plant the next day. They wanted to know if we could do an emergency run of 75,000 containers for their new product or should they consider another manufacturer."*

- **A:** *"I spent my lunch hour assembling a team that I knew could rise to the challenge. The six of us met later that day and developed an action plan. We figured out how to shift production from one line to another which had the side benefit of filling out a second shift schedule. I made calls to our vendors to line up raw materials and arrange JIT deliveries. The shop steward, who I had strategically added to the team, got excited about the project and organized the production plan and then helped me rearrange our shipping schedule so we wouldn't have any union issues."*

- **R:** *"When our customers arrived, they were blown away by our presentation and preparedness. They believed our claim that we could hit the 75,000 number was legitimate. As it turned out, we didn't get the business because the Food and Drug Administration began an industry-wide* *recall of the product, 80% of which came from counterfeiters in China. On the other hand, I was promoted in recognition of my organizing, planning, and team building skills."*

QUICK TIPS:
- Stories sell.
- Tell your story with energy and excitement.

Notes and Ideas

23. The Opening Interview Question

All too often, the first question you may be asked in an interview is, "So, tell me about yourself." I hate this question! Why? It's a lazy way to start an interview.

Okay, so this dreadful opening question has been asked. Let's make the best of it and make it work for you.

I suggest trying to think of yourself as a trial attorney on a TV legal show wherein this question represents your opening argument. The manner in which you answer this question will go a long way to setting the tone for your trial (interview).

Your response should be positive, upbeat, and short. See the example below. In her defense, HR-Heather may not ask this question, but you should expect it from the hiring manager. Consider several reasons for this:

1) First, interviewing may not be a comfortable activity for your future boss. This is an easy way for him or her to start the interview.

2) Second, she or he may not ever have seen your resume prior to your meeting and is playing

catch-up. In any case, try to make it easy your future boss by taking the high road and indulging him or her in the offense.

Don't be afraid to be the first person to speak. You can start the conversation (your goal is to have a conversation, not an interview) by asking a question about something in the office. Perhaps there are dead animals or fish on the wall. Look to see if there are pictures of whitewater rafting or skydiving. Are there awards or other civic recognition plaques on the desk? Avoid comments about the happy family photos, as this opens the door for the interviewer to ask questions about your family, which is a real no-no. (Remember the illegal interview questions listed in Chapter 17.) You can always ask about the company based on a recent news story or something unique in the lobby. The point is, you've started the conversation.

> **Note:**
> Karen, one of my job search colleagues and a lawyer, advises that even if this question is not asked, find a way to make your opening argument (statement). This will help you set the tone for the conversation and convey information you want to make sure gets on the table.

Question? What if he does ask the "tell me about yourself" question at the start of your interview? Should you talk about personal or professional issues? There is some debate among job coaches as to the best way to approach this question. When in doubt, ask the interviewer and take your cues from his answer. If directed to go the more personal route, be careful not to get too close to comments that could lead to illegal questions (Again, review Chapter 17.) My default is to go the professional path, as noted below.

Finally, practice, practice, practice. Your answer should flow smoothly without sounding scripted or memorized. Review the following example Mike K. used for his interview and modify for your situation.

EXAMPLE:
(Numbers in parentheses are explained below.)

> *"Thank you. (1) Let me say at the outset I am very excited to be here and learn more about the Manager of Engineering position. (2)*
>
> *Growing up on a farm (3) I've always had an interest in things mechanical which led me to Purdue (4), where I earned my BSME. (5)*
>
> *Over the past 15 (6) years, my career has taken me from a Fortune 500 implement manufacturer to*

Fortune 50 company and currently to international medical products company (7) *where I also earned my MBA.* (8)

I am particularly interested in process improvement. (9) *Am I right in assuming that is one of the major challenges* (10) *you are trying to address in this position?* (11)

EXPLANATION:

(1) Gratitude and appreciation are always a good opener.

(2) Confirm the position. Often things change between when the position description was issued and interviews began. Ask if there is any doubt.

(3) This gets close to violating the personal information caution, but sharing information, like being an Army brat, born in a foreign country, and home-schooled can lead to unique conversation. Just be careful.

(4) Share your education as a way to establish credentials and likely before the hiring manager gets to the second page of your resume.

(5) Affirm you are degreed.

(6) Adding a number here can be a double-edged sword. Think about it and include if it will help.

(7) Name dropping isn't always bad and will help the reader see those highlights on your resume.

(8) Adding an advanced degree or certifications shows you are a life-long learner.

(9) Shows your areas of interest.

(10) Confirm the major objectives or focus of the position. You might have incorrect assumptions or the hiring manager may have a different perspective.

(11) End with a question. This engages the interviewer and asks the other person to respond to you. It turns the interview into a conversation.

QUICK TIPS:

- Make "tell me about yourself" work for you.

- Practice, practice, practice.

24. The Closing Interview Question

If the opening interview question is often, "So tell me about yourself" (*Uggh!*), the closing interview question may be, "Why should I hire you?"

Continuing the legal analogy cited previously, this is the closing argument in your case (e.g., interview). Therefore, it needs punch, brevity, and memorability. It is critical that even if this question is not asked directly by the interviewer, think of a way to bring it into the conversation. This is your last, best shot at leaving a positive impression. Don't miss your chance.

Below is a sample closing statement with footnotes. Customize your answer to meet the specifics of your situation.

Again, be sure to give the same information to everyone you meet. You may get tired of repeating the same narrative three or four times but when the interview team meets, you want them all to have heard the same story. If you change or modify answers depending on the interviewer, you have introduced questions, and potentially fatal doubt, in their minds.

Finally, practice, practice, practice. Your answer should be well rehearsed, sincere, and thoughtful though not come across as scripted. I have borrowed Peter J.'s example. Notice the length.

EXAMPLE:
(Numbers in parentheses are explained below.)

> *"I want to express my appreciation for the opportunity to meet with you and to learn more about your company. (1) I am also impressed with the quality of the team you have built. (2)*
>
> *The Manager of Engineering Quality position we've been exploring (3) is a unique, and exciting, challenge for which I am well qualified. (4)*
>
> *As we have discussed, I have a broad engineering, as well as management, background (5) at Global Products Company (6) and my process improvement initiative (7) resulted in an annual savings of $12 million (8).*
>
> *I understand the urgency (9) of your process improvement goals (10) and can start delivering results (11) in the next 90 days (12).*

I'm really looking forward to being part of your team (13). Do you have any questions about my background that I didn't fully explain? (14) Where do we go from here? (15)"

EXPLANATION:

(1) Always say thank you.

(2) A little flattery is appropriate particularly if the team reports to the hiring manager. Shows you respect her judgment. This also affirms your own people assessment skills.

(3) Confirm the position for which you are interviewing. You don't know how many open positions the hiring manager is trying to fill or how many people she has interviewed.

(4) Reaffirm that you are qualified.

(5) Confirm the breadth of your skills particularly if managerial experience is involved and required for the position.

(6) Name dropping of a former employer may enhance your credibility and distinguish you from other candidates.

(7) Highlight your experience as it relates specifically to one of her current needs.

(8)   Showing you deliver and can quantify results is memorable. Don't overuse data as most of us can't remember too many numbers and you want your key accomplishment to stand out.

(9)   You understand her needs and are reminding her of their urgency.

(10)   Remind her of the specific skill or experience that qualifies you for this position.

(11)   You deliver results. See #7.

(12)   If your assessment leads you to believe you can deliver within a schedule, go for it. Don't say it if it's not true. You don't want to appear naïve or a braggart.

(13)   Shows enthusiasm for the job.

(14)   Gives the interviewer and you a chance to clarify any uncertainties or highlight any relevant topics.

(15)   Ask for the job!!! Short of that, find out what steps are next in the process. Don't leave things up in the air. Get a commitment to move forward.

QUICK TIPS:

- Make your case.

- Focus on impact and brevity.

- Practice, practice, practice.

.

Section 4
Approaching the Finish Line

Richard Longabaugh

Notes and Ideas

25. The Offer

You've made it this far. You've got an offer. Are you prepared to back away?

I realize this is counter-intuitive but now is not the time to go giddy. We'll take a look at some of the critical aspects of *The Offer*, but first things first.

Throughout this book, we have taken special care to note the emotional state of the job seeker. As stated in Chapter 5, job search is a roller-coaster ride. You are not at the end of your search and now is not the time to lose control. To reference our previous sports analogy, you have been running a marathon and the finish line may be in sight, but you still have some ground to cover, so don't blow it now.

For the first time on this journey, the balance of power has shifted in your direction. Consider that the company has invested a tremendous amount of time and dollars to find the right candidate. *You.* The last thing they want to do is to start the process all over again. You are the preferred candidate, and they are now motivated to do everything they can to get you on board.

The temptation for job seekers to accept the first offer is strong, particularly if they have been out of the game for a protracted period. Financial stress, family considerations, and professional stature are very real and can exert tremendous pressure. This is understandable but may be short-sighted.

At this point, the best thing to do is ***nothing***. Stop. Wait. Step back. The rationale for this posture is solid. The sobering fact is that not all offers should be accepted and it takes courage to decline an offer that does not meet your needs. Keep your emotions in check and approach this part of the process with sober rationalization.

Assuming your gut tells you everything about the company and this opportunity are good, let's consider next steps. You probably have been given a verbal offer that the company wants to hire you. Congratulations!

Do not accept.

Instead, tell the company you are pleased it wants you to join the team, but your acceptance is ***pending receipt of a written offer***. DO NOT waver on this step!

This is a very reasonable request and the employer should expect it. The company should also expect that when you get it, via e-mail or snail mail, that you will request some time to review the offer. A weekend is good but more than a few days is not. This is not gamesmanship on your part; rather, you should take this time to study every aspect of the offer and share it with your spouse, advisor, or attorney.

Let me pause to offer some coaching to make sure you are in the right frame of mind. As we have previously referenced, job seekers often feel (wrongly) they are damaged goods by virtue of their unemployment status (temporary) and have to take a lower salary or lesser position as penance.

No! No! No!

When someone comes to my groups and announces he or she has received a job offer, one question I always ask "Is the salary at, above, or below your previous position?" I can honestly report that more than 70 percent of job seekers end up with a higher salary and better job than their previous position. Don't settle for less because you think you have to.

With a written job offer in hand, now is the time for some serious deliberation. When should you determine what you want in an offer? Answer—at the beginning of your search. You should have taken the time to seriously consider what is important to you right after you got *The Boot.* I alerted you to this back in Chapter 2.

If there is something in the offer which doesn't make sense or meet your expectations, you should determine if this is 1) simply a matter of clarification or 2) is it something you need to negotiate. However, it is not a given that you, or the employer, are expected to negotiate. If you have done your homework and had candid discussions throughout the interview process, most offer conversations go very smoothly and you may find there is nothing to negotiate.

However, if there are reasons to discuss certain points in the offer, know who you need to contact—HR-Heather or the hiring manager.

> ***Secret Tip:***
> ***It may be somewhat tougher negotiating higher levels of salary and benefits with HR-Heather. On the other hand, the hiring manager is eager to have you get started and may be more inclined to accommodate your requests.***

There are numerous components in an offer and you should consider the offer in its totality. Too many people stop at salary without considering, for example, how much you may have to contribute for healthcare insurance. Regarding salary, if you have done your homework (Chapter 19) and had discussions about salary during your interviews, you should not be surprised by the offer.

On the other hand, if you did not get what you wanted, ask for an increase based on what your research shows is standard for the position in this industry. If still denied, don't lose hope. There may be several components of the offer that offset the higher salary you are seeking. Look carefully and determine their dollar value to you.

It's important to keep in mind that companies have different buckets (or budgets) from which they pay their employees. Salaries are often departmental expenses,

> **Secret Tip:**
> One of the easiest benefits to negotiate is an increase in vacation. In all likelihood, it will not adversely impact the boss's departmental budget, which makes it easy for him to give it away. Also, don't be afraid to negotiate trade-offs. If you don't need health insurance, ask for the premium in a salary adjustment.

whereas health insurance may be in a separate company-wide bucket.

Below is a list of some of the items you should review before accepting an offer. The list is not exhaustive but many are standard in a company's benefit programs. You owe it to yourself to ask about them.

- Signing bonus
- 90-day performance review and salary adjustment
- Annual bonus/profit sharing details
- Quarterly bonus
- Life and health insurance programs and cost
- Long term disability
- 401k match
- Cell phone and computer reimbursement

- Car allowance

- Vacation, PTO and sick time

- Education benefits

- Industry conferences and trade show attendance

- Business travel reimbursement and charge cards

If you are happy with the tweaks in the offer, accept it and set a start date. If you are not satisfied and there is no room for compromising, then you must politely reject the offer. This is one of hardest things to do in job search, but if you find you have made too many concessions, you will never be happy in your job. I cannot recall a single case of a job seeker regretting the tough decision to turn down an unacceptable offer.

COMPETING OFFERS

After all your efforts to get an offer, don't be surprised if your diligence has yielded two, or more, offers at the same time. It happens more often than you might guess so you should be prepared. To a limited extent, you may be able to leverage one against the other, but don't count on it. This tactic can quickly turn to resentment and a rescinded offer.

The best way to handle this situation is with transparency and honesty. During your interviews, make HR-Heather and the hiring manager aware that you are active in job search and have several active prospects. Don't get coy or cute. Keep them apprised of your search progress and let them know when you get another offer. At the very least, you may be able to get them to speed up their decision making. Perhaps you can leverage yourself to a higher offer.

QUICK TIPS:

- Stay in control.

- Don't settle for a bad offer.

- Clarify and negotiate as needed.

Notes and Ideas

Notes and Ideas

26. References

Undoubtedly, you have seen an ad for a position that says send cover letter, resume, salary history, and three references. What do you do?

DO NOT send the references!

Politely say, "References will be provided at a later date." If you get push-back and your application will not be processed without the references, consider contacting the company directly or withdrawing your application. You never want someone contacting your references without your knowledge and permission, particularly if you have not yet been interviewed.

References are an undervalued, yet highly critical, component of your presentation. Unfortunately, employers can be way too casual when it comes to references. Some don't even check them. When I did retained executive searches, I went through reference interviews on my leading candidate typically lasting more than an hour and asking as many as 40 questions. Granted, that is unusual.

How should you approach the reference portion of your candidacy and why not provide them upfront?

Let me begin by saying: Don't wait until the end of the interview process to start working on your references. You should have a stable of six to ten references lined up and ready to go about the time you start doing face-to-face interviews. However, do not feel pressured to provide names until you are certain this is a job you want and then, only when asked. You need to maintain control of this part of the process.

Ask the hiring manager, "What do you want to know?" Does he want to confirm accomplishments, specific details, character traits, managerial abilities, interpersonal skills or something else? You will only find out if you ask. Depending on the reply, select the references who can best provide the insights the hiring manager is seeking. This assures you of the best chance to have references who will enhance your candidacy. To be clear, we are not talking about your pastor, brother-in-law, or next-door neighbor.

Let's step back and address the six to ten numbers mentioned above. Are you going to give all the names? No. Like a baseball manager deciding who to send up to the plate, this is your bench and you will select only those references who will give the hiring manager the best perspective for the issues he has raised.

Preparing your references in advance is important. In building your reference team, contact individuals you think might be in a position to speak on your behalf. Let them know you are in a job search and might wish to use them as references. Show them the courtesy of asking permission to have a prospective employer contact them. Tell them that if an opportunity presents itself, you will call them first.

When you are asked to provide references and know the hiring manager's areas of interest, ask how many people he would like to contact and when a reference is likely to get a call. Make sure you know who is going to make the call—the hiring manager or HR-Heather.

Before giving any names, call the individual references and brief them on the position for which you are a candidate and what the hiring manager is likely to ask. Then give the names and contact information to the hiring manager.

Ask your references to call you after they have been contacted and share what was discussed and if they detect any lingering doubts on the part of the hiring manager.

Finally, send them thank-you notes and commit to letting them know what happens in your search.

QUICK TIPS:
- Maintain control of the process.
- Be deliberate giving reference names.
- Brief your references in advance.

Richard Longabaugh

Notes and Ideas

27. Follow-up

Congratulations! You did it!

But you didn't do it alone. There are many people and organizations to thank. Your log or journal will help you remember all those who should be singled out for helping you along this journey. You know who they are and whether they should get a call, email, or a hand-written note (the best). Get started on the thank-you notes before you begin your new job.

Now that you are back among the wage-earners, let me suggest how you should plan to spend some of that new income. If there are groups or organizations who gave you a free membership while you were unemployed, join and pay the dues. In the case of the networking organizations that supported you, most of them are nonprofits like churches. Make a donation to help them in their mission just as they helped you.

No doubt you now appreciate the value of networking. Solidify your contacts on LinkedIn or other networks. Let them know you have landed. Promise yourself you will refresh your network regularly and don't let it get stale or atrophy. You never know when you might need to activate the network again and it could be useful in your new job.

Your new employer will want you to start as soon as possible. Take a vacation or at least a long weekend. You need to clear your head from all the job-search commotion and start your new job with a fresh perspective.

Remember all those informational interviews and the contacts you made? You are now in a position to return the favor. If a job seeker contacts you in the future, TAKE THE CALL! You now know what it's like to be that person on the other end of the line. Make the time to repay the kindness others gave to you when you needed their help.

QUICK TIP:

- Say thank you.

- Pay it forward.

28. In Closing

I hope this book has been helpful in your job search. Job searching is not an easy endeavor. I know. I've been there twice in my career. I wish I could tell you there is a secret path to finding a new job if you do A, B, and C, or follow a specific program. Unfortunately, there is no secret, nor is there a substitute for the hard work it takes. You need to stay the course and have faith you will be successful.

The advice and counsel offered herein represents collective wisdom and insights gained from the painful struggles of the many job seekers and managers I have known.

Some of my suggestions may not work for you but I can promise you they are all real-world tested and steps that have been part of successful job searches for many others in the past.

Thank you for putting up with my brash tone and sometimes convoluted writing style. I hope you got at least one good idea. Please feel free to write and let me know of your job search experiences.

Good luck and happy hunting!

Appendix 1
THE FIVE STAGES OF GRIEF MODEL
By Elisabeth Kubler-Ross

1) DENIAL

Denial is a conscious or unconscious refusal to accept facts, information, reality, etc. relating to the situation concerned. It's a defense mechanism and perfectly natural. Some people can become locked in this stage when dealing with a traumatic change that cannot be ignored.

2) ANGER

Anger can manifest in different ways. People dealing with emotional upset can be angry with themselves and/or with others, especially those close to them. Knowing this helps keep one detached and non-judgmental when experiencing the anger of someone who is very upset.

3) BARGAINING

Traditionally, the bargaining stage for people facing death can involve attempting to bargain with whatever God the person believes in. People facing less serious trauma can bargain or seek to negotiate compromise. For example, "Can we still be friends?..." when facing a break-up. Bargaining rarely provides a sustainable solution.

4) DEPRESSION

Also referred to as preparatory grieving. In a way, it's the dress rehearsal or the practice run for the "aftermath" although this stage means different things depending on whom it involves. It's a sort of acceptance with emotional attachment. It's natural to feel sadness and regret, fear, uncertainty, etc. It shows that the person has at least begun to accept the reality.

5) ACCEPTANCE

Again, this stage definitely varies according to the person's situation, although broadly, it is an indication that there is some emotional detachment and objectivity.

(Based on the Grief Cycle model first published in *On Death and Dying*, Elisabeth Kubler-Ross, 1969.)

Appendix 2

JOB SEARCH & SPECIALTY WEBSITES

Note: Internet sites come and go and others may have changed their name. Do not rely on the accuracy of this list. You are responsible for your own research.

JOB OPPORTUNITIES

http://lhhus.careers.adicio.com/careers/user/login

http://hotjobs.yahoo.com

http://www.4jobs.com

http://www.brassring.com

http://www.careerbank.com

http://www.careerbuilder.com

http://www.careerjournal.com

http://www.careernet.com

http://www.careers.excite.com

http://www.craigslist.com

http://www.csolutionsgroup.com

http://www.employment911.com

http://www.employmentguide.com

http://www.globalrecruiters.com

http://www.ejobfairs.net

http://www.guru.com/pro/professional

http://www.hotjobs.com

http://www.indeed.com

http://www.ipa.com

http://www.intelligencecareers.com

http://www.job.com

http://www.jobboardinfo.com

http://www.jobdig.com

http://www.jobfox.com

http://www.jobfly.com

http://www.jobstar.org

http://www.jobsonline.net

http://www.job-hunt.org

http://www.monster.com

http://www.nationalcareerfairs.com

http://www.quincareers.com

http://www.recruitersonline.com

http://www.resumespider.com

http://www.simplyhired.com

http://www.sologig.com

http://www.thingamajob.com

http://www.topjobsites.com

http://www.wantedjobs.com

http://www.webhire.com

50-PLUS JOB SITES

http://www.encore.org

http://www.retiredbrains.com

http://www.retirementjobs.com

ASSOCIATIONS

http://www.asaenet.org

http://www.weddles.com/associations/index.htm

http://www.gsae.org http://www.idealist.org

ENERGY

http://www.energyjobs.com

http://www.energyinfosource.com

http://www.greencareercentral.com/public/main.cfm

EXECUTIVE

http://www.6figurejobs.com

http://www.6figures.com

http://www.bluesteps.com

http://www.ceoupdate.com

http://www.cfo.com/careers/?f=header

http://www.executiveopenings.com

http://www.execunet.com

http://online.wsj.com/public/page/news-career-jobs.html

http://www.sixfigurejobs.com

http://www.theladders.com

http://www.chiefmonster.com

http://www.execusearches.com

http://www.implu.com

http://www.boardnet.usa.org

FEDERAL, GOVERNMENT & SECURITY CLEARANCE

http://www.jobsfed.com

http://www.usajobs.opm.gov

http://www.federaltimes.com

http://www.avuecentral.com

http://www.makingthedifference.org

http://www.bestplacestowork.org

http://www.resume-place.com/

http://www.gpoaccess.gov/plumbook/index.html

http://www.corporategrayonline.com

http://www.ourpublicservice.org http://www.bls.gov

http://www.jobcentral.com

http://www.washingtontechnology.com

http://www.usaspending.com

http://www.govcon.com

http://www.opm.gov/ses

FINANCE

http://www.afsc-jobs.com

http://www.bankjobs.com

http://www.finacialjobs.com

http://www.fjn.com

http://www.jobsinthemoney.com

http://www.nbfsearch.com

http://www.nbn-jobs.com

http://www.bloomberg.com

http://www.financialjobnetwork.com

http://www.jobsinthemoney.com

http://www.efinancialcareers.com/

http://www.jobsonwallstreet.com

http://www.cfo.com

http://www.mava.org

HEALTHCARE / PHARMACEUTICAL & BIOTECH

http://www.bio.com

http://www.biofind.com

http://www.biospace.com

http://www.bioview.com

http://www.hcrnetwork.com

http://www.healthcareers.com

http://www.healthleaders.com

http://www.jobsinhealthcare.com

http://www.medhunters.com

http://www.pharmhire.com

http://www.rxcareercenter.com/

http://www.Hirehealth.com

http://www.adsumo.com

http://www.bmn.com

http://www.medsearch.com

http://www.medzilla.com

http://www.recap.com

HOSPITALITY

http://www.hcareers.com

http://www.hospitalityrecruiters.com

http://www.hospitalityonline.com

HUMAN RESOURCES

http://www.ere.net

http://www.hrworld.com

http://www.shrm.org

http://www.ihire.com

http://www.thehrsource.com

http://www.mmshrm.org/JobBank/jobOpenings.asp

JOURNALISM

http://www.journalismnext.com

http://www.asne.org

http://www.icfj.org

http://www.nna.org

http://www.writersdigest.com

http://www.publishersweekly.com

http://www.journalismjobs.com

http://www.nwu.org

http://www.naa.org

MARKETING

http://www.marketingjobs.com

http://www.marketproinc.com

http://www.WomenSportsJobs.com

http://www.mbaglobalnet.com

http://www.mbajungle.com

http://www.mbatalentwire.com

MEDIA & ENTERTAINMENT

http://www.meetup.com

http://www.mediabistro.com

http://www.mpaa.org

http://www.sologigs.com

http://www.afi.com

http://www.afci.org

NON-PROFIT

http://www.fdncenter.org/pnd/jobs

http://www.foundationscenter.org

http://www.guidestar.org

http://www.nonprofit-jobs.org

http://www.goodmoney.com/jobs.htm

http://www.philanthropy.com

http://www.chronicle.com

http://www.ncna.org

http://www.nptimes.com/Feb04/specialreport.pdf

http://www.idealist.org

http://www.guidestar.org/

PROJECT MANAGEMENT

http://www.projectmanager.com

http://www.pmi.org

RETAIL

http://www.allretailjobs.com

SOCIOLOGISTS

http://www.assanet.org

TECHNOLOGY

http://www.dice.com

http://www.at-tech.com

http://www.fiberopticsonline.com

http://www.itcareers.com

http://www.ithotjobs.com/

http://www.techjobbank.com

http://www.telecomcareers.net

http://www.itools.com

http://www.directionsmag.com

http://www.elance.com

http://www.computerjobs.com

http://www.lightreading.com

http://www.ThinkJobs.com

http://www.wired.com

http://www.redherring.com

JOB SEARCH WEBSITES

http://www.theladders.com

http://www.recruiterconnection.com

http://www.execunet.com

http://www.executivesonly.com

http://www.vicepresidentsjobs.com

http://www.resumedirector.com

http://www.resumerabbit.com

http://www.bluesteps.com -

http://www.executive.computerjobs.com

http://www.ritesite.com –

BUSINESS CARDS

http://www.vistaprint.com

http://www.123print.com

http://www.quintcareers.com/networking_
    businesscards.html

http://www.mossbaysoftware.com

http://www.zazzle.com

COMPANY INFO/RESEARCH

http://www.lead411.com/top-companies-list.taf

http://money.cnn.com/magazines/fortune/fortune500/

HEALTH INSURANCE

http://www.ehealthinsurance.com

http://www.consumer.eassurance.com

http://www.ejsmith.com □ http://www.anthem.com
http://www.aetna.com
http://www.bcbs.com

JOB TRAINING

http://www.trainingcamp.com
http://www.gcflearnfree.org
http://www.worklife.com/
http://www.crn.com
http://www.microsoft.com

LOCAL RESOURCES

http://ww2.wisconsin.gov/state/employment
http://www.wisconsinjobcenter.org
http://www.wisconsinjobnetwork.com
http://Wisconsin.jobing.com
http://www.nationjob.com/wisconsin

NETWORKING

http://www.linkedin.com
http://www.reunion.com
http://www.afcea.com
http://www.thefeng.com -
http://www.ryze.com
http://www.spoke.org
http://www.wng.com -
http://www.asbc.org

http://www.yescircle.org

http://www.mengonline.com

PUBLICATIONS

http://www.businessweek.com

http://www.blackenterprise.com

http://www.bloomberg.com

http://www.forbes.com

http://www.nbci.com

http://www.newspage.com

http://www.finance.yahoo.com/

http://www.interbiznet.com

http://www.workingmother.com

http://www.wrightinvestments.com

http://www.sciencemagazine.com

http://www.libraryspot.com

http://www.aarp.com

http://www.areacode-info.com

http://www.business.com

http://www.careerbook.com

http://www.potomactechwire.com

http://www.bizweb.com

http://www.inc.com/500

http://www.wsj.com

http://www.womenforhire.com

http://www.womenworking2000.com

http://www.myoptiovalue.com

http://www.sec.gov

http://www.onecenter.org

RELOCATION & MOVING

http://www.child.com/kids/health_nutrition/fittest_states.jsp

http://www.realtor.com

http://www.escapeartist.com

RESUMES

http://www.wordle.net/

http://www.visualcv.com

SALARY

http://www.cbsalary.com

http://www.salarysource.com □ http://www.compgeo.net

http://www.salaryexpert.com

http://www.salaryreviesa.com

http://www.wageweb.com

http://www.salary.com

http://www.moneycentral.msn.com/investor/home.asp

http://www.glassdoor.com

http://www.callfranklyspeaking.com/sallink.htm

http://www.bls.gov/data/home.htm

http://www.erieri.com

http://www.homefair.com/homefair/calc/salcalc.html

http://www.nolo.com/encyclopedia/articles/articles/emp/
    howmuch.html

http://www.salaryclock.com

SEARCH ENGINES

Altavista.com

Dogpile.com

Google.com

Looksmart.com

TheUltimates.com

Yahoo.com

DirectHit.com

Experiencenet.com

Hotbot.com

Metacrawler.com

Vivisimo.com

AllTheWeb.com Excite.com

Highway61.com

Lycos.com

Vault.com

Dmoz.org

Go.com

Isleuth.com

Northernlight.com

Wetfeet.com

UNEMPLOYMENT OFFICE

http://www.dwd.state.wi.us/uiben

ENTREPRENEUR AND GENERAL INFO

http://www.AllBusiness.com

http://www.bizstarters.com
http://www.entrepreneur.com
http://www.fwe.org
http://www.garage.com
http://www.Morebusiness.com
http://www.ipocentral.com
http://ir.infousa.com/
http://www.nase.org
http://www.score.org

FRANCHISES

http://www.theesource.com
http://www.frannet.com
http://www.franchoice.com

INSURANCE

http://www.hoaa.com/
http://www.jbsba.com/content/suites/hb_teleworking/
index.shtml -

BUSINESS PLANS

http://www.allbusiness.com/entrepreneurs_center/
        business_plans.html
http://www.bplans.com/
http://www.bizplanpro.com
http://www.sba.gov/starting_business/planning/basic.html
http://www.toolkit.cch.com/tolls/buspln_m.asp

STARTUPS

http://www.fastcompany.com

http://www.startupexecs.com

http://www.startupzone.com

http://www.topstartups.com

LEGAL & TAX

http://www.legalzoom.com

http://www.mycorporation.com

http://www.nolo.com

http://www.irs.gov/businesses/small

VENTURE CAPITAL

http://www.glocapsearch.com

http://www.siliconvalley.com

http://www.vfinance.com

http://www.vcbuzz.com

http://www.vfinance.com

About the Author

Richard Longabaugh has been coaching those who find themselves in the unfortunate circumstance of unemployment since the "Great Recession of 2008." Since those gray days, he has led more than 600 group meetings of job seekers and every year conducts more than 100 one-on-one coaching sessions.

In addition, he has been a business executive with hiring responsibilities, a retained executive search consultant for more than a dozen years, and has been unemployed— more than once. This background gives him unique insights when it comes to job search. Known as a demanding coach who preaches, "It's better to sweat, cry, and bleed in a networking group than on a job interview," Rich has compiled these collective experiences into some of the best advice available to job seekers. Agree or disagree with his tough-love, no-nonsense approach to finding a new job, the advice provided in this book is time-tested and has delivered results for hundreds of job seekers.

He asks, "Is losing your job the best thing that can happen to you?"

Contact information: authorrjl@gmail.com

www.ingramcontent.com/pod-product-compliance
Lightning Source LLC
Chambersburg PA
CBHW050825090426
42738CB00031B/3454